THE STORY OF THE CHOSEN PEOPLE

MOSES EXPOSED ON THE NILE

THE STORY OF THE CHOSEN PEOPLE

BY

H. A. GUERBER

YESTERDAY'S CLASSICS

CHAPEL HILL, NORTH CAROLINA

This edition, first published in 2009 by Yesterday's Classics, an imprint of Yesterday's Classics, LLC, is an unabridged republication of the text originally published by American Book Company in 1896. For the complete listing of the books that are published by Yesterday's Classics, please visit www.yesterdaysclassics.com. Yesterday's Classics is the publishing arm of the Baldwin Online Children's Literature Project which presents the complete text of hundreds of classic books for children at www.mainlesson.com.

ISBN-10: 1-59915-331-9

ISBN-13: 978-1-59915-331-5

Yesterday's Classics, LLC
PO Box 3418
Chapel Hill, NC 27515

PREFACE

In this little volume the author has tried to give a consecutive story of the Jews, or Chosen People, as objectively as the Stories of the Greeks and of the Romans, with which it forms a series. The narrative has been written in the simplest style, so as to enable even the youngest child of the third or fourth reader grade to understand it.

Not the least attempt has been made to dwell upon the strictly religious side of the subject, for, owing to the mixed population in our large cities and schools, such an attempt would be impracticable. The sole aim of this very elementary work is to familiarize children, be they of Jewish, Protestant, Roman Catholic, or Freethinker parentage, with the outline of the story contained in the Old Testament, so that they can understand the allusions which appear even in juvenile literature, and can look with intelligent appreciation upon the reproductions of works of art which are now to be found in nearly all our books and magazines.

I have found that, when told to young children, these historical narratives prove a source of much interest, and that the elementary knowledge then obtained remains so clear and vivid that even when they are grown up, and able to enter into the subject more thoroughly, the impression of the story as first heard is the one which is most permanent.

While it may seem that, with all the facilities which the country affords to rich and poor alike, such instruction in schools would be superfluous, the fact remains that, with the exception of a few well-known stories, the children have no idea of the contents of the Old Testament. This lack of general information on the subject is often a great drawback to teachers in the course of their instruction, as references are constantly made to the Bible.

Although this is a juvenile history of the Jews, it has not been written without much research; and, in order to make it as brief, comprehensive, and accurate as possible, many authorities beside the Bible, Josephus, and the Bible dictionaries, have been consulted.

It is hoped that an inkling of the story of the Jews will stimulate the children's interest, will early imbue them with a taste for history, and will give them the desire to gain further and more complete information on the subject when they grow older.

CONTENTS

Vicinity of Jerusalem Inset

Gibeon
Kirjath-jearim
Mizpeh
Gibeah
Anathoth
Nob
Scopus
Golgotha
Gethsemane
Mt. of Olives
Brook Kidron
JERUSALEM
Plain of Rephaim
Aqueduct
Bethany
Rachel's Tomb
Zelah
Bethlehem
Solomon's Pool
Etam

VICINITY OF JERUSALEM
SCALE, 8 MILES TO THE INCH

The Holy Land

36
34
33
32
32
35
36

GREAT SEA
PHŒNICIA
NAPHTALI
LEBANON MT.
ANTI-LIBANUS
BEYOND JORDAN
MANASSEH
Sidon
Sarepta
Tyre
Achzib
Kadesh
Waters of Merom
Dan or Laish
Mt. Hermon
DAMASCUS
Accho
Bethsaida
Capernaum
Sea of Galilee or Tiberias
Tiberias
Mt. Carmel
Mt. Tabor
ZEBULON
Nazareth
Kanah
Endor
ISSACHAR
Dor
Jezreel
Caesarea
Gilgal
MANASSEH
GAD
SHARON
SAMARIA
Samaria
Shechem
Tirzah
Ramoth-Gilead
Joppa
EPHRAIM
Libnah
Shiloh
Jephtha-Ammonites
Rabbath Ammon
Bethel
Jericho
BENJAMIN
JERUSALEM
Bethabara
REUBEN
Ashdod
Samuel-Philistines
Askelon
Gath
David-Goliath
Bethlehem
Adullam
Mt. Nebo
Gaza
PHILISTINES
SIMEON
JUDAH
Hebron
Goshen
Beersheba
DEAD SEA
1292 ft. below Sea Level
MOABITES
MIDIANITES
River Jordan
MEDITERRANEAN SEA

THE HOLY LAND

SCALE: 40 MILES PER INCH
0   10   20   30   40

CHAPTER I

THE CREATION

THE Bible, as you already know, is composed of two parts, called the Old and the New Testaments. Both Jews and Christians consider that the first part of this book is sacred, because it contains God's teachings as he revealed, or made them known, to man. They do not, however, agree about the second part, which is considered sacred only by Christians.

The Old Testament contains, besides God's teachings, a history of the Jews, which is so interesting and important that educated people of all countries and religions are expected to know all about it. It is this history which you are going to hear, but, of course, if you want it complete, you must read it in the Bible itself.

The very first book of the Bible is called Genesis, a word meaning "origin," because it tells us about the beginning, or origin, of the world. We are told that in the beginning there was neither land nor water, nor any living things, and that darkness rested over all.

This early stage of affairs, when the elements of all things were mixed up together, has been called Chaos (confusion); and we are told that God, the Almighty,

1

who had no beginning or end, created, or made, the whole world out of Chaos.

The story is told very briefly indeed, and all the periods of creation are called days. Of course we now know that by days the writer of the book of Genesis did not mean twenty-four hours, as we do. The word "days" was used for an indefinite space of time; and, just as God is far more powerful than we can imagine, so his days are far longer than ours.

God's spirit moved over Chaos, and during the first day he said: "Let there be light." At these words the darkness which rested over all things vanished, and light first appeared. This light shone through the thick vapors which then surrounded the earth.

During the second day, or period, the vapors parted, and now for the first time the blue sky could mirror itself in the blue waters which covered the face of the earth. As the clouds in the sky could rain down water, the Bible says that on the second day God "divided the waters which were under the firmament [or sky] from the waters which were above the firmament."

During the third day, or period, another great change took place; for the crust of the earth, shaken by earthquakes, formed great bumps and hollows. Thus were formed mountains and valleys; and the waters, which had covered all the face of the earth, now flowed into the deep basins, where they formed lakes, seas, and oceans.

As soon as dry land appeared, God said that the earth should bring forth grass, trees, and plants of all kinds; and each one was to have seeds, so that new plants would replace the old as soon as they died. The earth had been bare and ugly when it first rose up out of the waters; but it was now covered with verdure, and became beautiful as it is to-day.

On the fourth day, God allowed the lights in the sky to be seen; and the sun, moon, and stars began to serve, as they do now, to mark the days and the nights, the seasons and the years. Darkness and light were thus clearly divided, and we are told that "God saw that it was good."

During the fifth day, or period, when the rays of the sun had strengthened the trees and plants, God created the birds and fishes, and bade them multiply and fly through the air, and fill all the waters in the seas. It is in obedience to this command that the birds and fishes lay eggs and hatch their young.

The sixth day, or period, was spent in the creation of the higher animals, and lastly of man. Now the Bible tells us that man was formed out of earth, but that he was different from all the beings which had already been created, because he was like God.

This first man bore the name of Adam. Although his body was made of dust, his life was breathed into him by God, who brought all the animals to him that he might name them, and told him that he should be master over them all.

God had labored for six whole days, or periods, and from Chaos had brought forth the world and all the living creatures in it. He gazed upon his work, "saw everything that he had made, and behold, it was very good." The labor was done, so, on the seventh day, God "rested from all his work."

It is partly because God rested on the seventh day, after laboring six days, that we work for six days of the week, and rest on the seventh; and each Sunday is thus an anniversary of God's day of rest.

CHAPTER II

THE FORBIDDEN FRUIT

ADAM had been placed in a beautiful garden named Eden, which God had planted, and which was watered by four rivers. Here God came to visit the first man, and told him that he could eat of the fruit of every plant and tree in the garden, except the fruit which grew on "the tree of the knowledge of good and evil." This tree was placed in the center of the garden, and God gave this order to find out whether Adam would obey him.

Besides, if the man did not eat of the fruit, he would never know trouble or sickness. At the same time that God gave this first command, or law, he added the first punishment, or penalty, saying: "For in the day that thou eatest thereof thou shalt surely die."

God now brought the animals which he had created, so that Adam might name them all. In doing so, the man saw that the beasts went about in pairs, and that he was the only living creature who had no mate. He felt very lonely when he saw this, and told God that he would like to have a companion like himself. So the Creator "caused a deep sleep to fall upon Adam, and he slept; and he took one of his ribs," and from it made a woman.

When Adam awoke, God brought the first woman to him. Adam saw that she was a part of himself; and he said that a man shall "leave his father and mother, and shall cleave unto his wife." Thus, in the Garden of Eden and in the presence of God himself, the first marriage was celebrated; and Adam and his wife were so pure and innocent that they were perfectly happy, and no more ashamed of being naked than little children.

Adam dwelt in the Garden of Eden with Eve, as the first woman was called, in perfect happiness, which was to last as long as they obeyed God and did not eat any of the fruit which hung on "the tree of the knowledge of good and evil." Unfortunately, however, there was an evil spirit, called the Tempter, the Devil, or Satan, who entered the Garden of Eden in the form of a serpent.

He was jealous of the happiness of Adam and Eve, and very anxious to deprive them of it. So he spoke to Eve, and told her that God had forbidden their eating any of the fruit of the tree in the center of the garden only because he wanted to keep it all for himself.

The serpent then urged Eve to taste the fruit, saying: "Ye shall not surely die; for God doth know that in the day ye eat thereof, then your eyes shall be opened, and ye shall be as gods, knowing good and evil." Eve believed the words of the wicked serpent, ate some of the fruit, and gave some to Adam, who ate it too.

As the serpent had said, their eyes were now opened; and, whereas they had known only good before, they now knew evil also. God had seen that they would never be perfectly happy if they knew evil, and he had kindly kept that knowledge from them.

But now they had disobeyed his command, and with the knowledge of evil came the feeling of shame and fear, which they had never had before, and which made them go and hide among the trees of the garden. In the cool of the day, God came into the garden, and called to them. Adam came slowly, in answer to this call, and excused himself, saying that he was afraid to come out because he was naked.

At these words, God asked him whether he had tasted the forbidden fruit; and when Adam confessed that the woman had given him some, God questioned Eve. She, in her turn, confessed her disobedience, but said that the serpent had tempted her.

Both Adam and Eve had broken the first law, so they had to suffer the punishment which God had warned them they must receive. The serpent, who had tempted the woman, was condemned to be hated of all men, and to crawl in the dust. Eve was told that she must obey her husband, and that she would suffer, while Adam was doomed to a life of hard work, because the earth would no longer yield him food unless he tilled the soil.

No promise was added to make the serpent's sentence less severe, but Eve was told that her children would fight against the serpent (the spirit of evil), and that in time one of them would conquer him. Adam was promised that his toil would not be in vain, but that God would bless it and enable him to earn, by the sweat of his brow, the bread without which he could not live.

When the judgment against the serpent, the man, and the woman had thus been given, God reminded Adam and Eve that, as they had sinned, they would suffer death. He warned them that as their bodies had been made of dust, they could not last forever, using the words which are now spoken in the funeral service: "Dust thou art, and unto dust shalt thou return."

CHAPTER III

THE FIRST MURDER

GOD is as good as he is just, so he next taught Adam and Eve how to clothe themselves in the skins of wild beasts, and then sent them out of the Garden of Eden, which they were never to see again. God did not want them to come back there, because the tree of life grew in the garden, and as long as they ate of its fruit they could not die. To prevent their coming in again, he placed an angel at the gates of Paradise (Eden), and armed him with a flaming sword which turned every way.

Although Adam and Eve suffered keenly for their disobedience, they did not despair. They believed God's words, and began to look forward to the time when the promised child would come, who, by killing the serpent, would make up for the harm they had done. The mention of this child is the first prophecy about the Messiah, or Redeemer; and from the day she left Eden, Eve lived in constant hope of his coming. To prevent man from forgetting this promise, and, the Christians say, as a sign of the last great sacrifice in the Bible, God also taught Adam and Eve to offer living animals upon his altar.

It was after they had been driven out of Eden that Eve gave birth to her first child, in sorrow and suffering, as God had foretold. This child was called Cain, a word which means "a possession," because his mother thought that he was the promised child; but when her second son, Abel, meaning "a breath or vapor," was born, Eve began to understand that the time for the keeping of God's promise might still be a long way off.

While Eve nursed her children, Adam tilled the soil, and when the two boys grew up, they worked too, Cain at the plow, and Abel as a shepherd. Thus, you see, farming and cattle raising were the two first occupations of man.

When these two young men were old enough, they got ready to offer a sacrifice to God. But Cain, the elder, was in a bad temper when he laid a basket of fruit on the altar. An offering made in such a spirit could not be agreeable to God, so he not only refused it, but also rebuked Cain for his bad feelings. Abel, who was gentle and loving, brought a lamb from his flock, and laid it upon the altar, full of love and trust in God; so his sacrifice was accepted.

Shortly after this ceremony, the two brothers met in a very lonely place; and Cain, who had long been jealous of his brother, took this chance to fall upon him and murder him. This first crime was very quickly punished. Even as Cain fled in terror from the spot where his brother's lifeless body was lying, God suddenly appeared to him, and asked: "Where is Abel, thy brother?"

DEATH OF ABEL

Cain crossly answered: "Am I my brother's keeper?" But God knew all that had happened. To punish Cain, God told him that the earth would no longer bear any fruit under his care, and that he would not be allowed to make his home near the spot where his murdered brother lay.

At the same time, God also filled Cain's heart with a constant dread that some one would kill him, as he had killed Abel. He therefore fled in terror; but God, who did not wish him to perish, put a mark upon him, and spoke a sevenfold curse upon any one who should dare to lay hands upon him.

Protected by this mysterious mark, which is called the "brand of Cain," the unhappy man started out; and, after wandering about in an aimless way for some time, he settled in the land of Nod, a word which means "banishment."

Here Cain saw that the earth would no longer bring forth fruit for his support; so he ceased to earn his living as a farmer, and began to make all kinds of things instead. His haunting fears, however, never left him; and

to protect himself, he built a fortified city, to which he gave the name of his son Enoch.

We know very little about Cain's life after that, and the Bible only tells us the names of some of his descendants. Lamech, his great-great-great grandson, was the father of Jabal, the first wandering herdsman, and Jubal, the inventor of the first musical instruments, and Tubal-cain, the first smith, who made articles of iron and bronze.

CHAPTER IV

THE DELUGE

ADAM and Eve, in the mean while, continued to live alone, mourning the death of Abel, and the departure of Cain. But when they were one hundred and thirty years old, a third son was born to them, and they called him Seth, which means "the appointed," because they thought that it was surely the Redeemer who had come.

They were again disappointed, however; but Seth married, and Adam had many descendants, the sixth in direct line being Enoch. This man was very good and pious, and "walked with God." He was rewarded for his goodness; for God did not allow him to die like the rest of his race, but carried him off to heaven, so that "he should not see death."

Enoch's son, Methuselah, is noted as having reached the greatest age ever attained by man,—nine hundred and sixty-nine years. He was two hundred and forty-three years old when Adam died, and must often have heard him tell about the Garden of Eden, the eating of the forbidden fruit, and how he was driven out of Paradise.

Methuselah's grandson was Noah, who was born six hundred years before Methuselah died; and Noah no doubt often heard his grandfather relate the stories which Adam had told.

The world had grown very wicked during the fifteen hundred and fifty-six years which had passed by since the creation of Adam; for his numerous descendants had married daughters of Cain, and had learned to do many evil things.

When God saw that the people were growing so bad, he no longer allowed them to become as old as their fathers had lived to be. Instead of permitting men to live nearly a thousand years, like the good Methuselah, God shortened their lives.

Then, a little later, seeing that the "wickedness of man was great in the earth," God regretted having ever created man, and made up his mind to take the human race off the face of the earth, and completely destroy it. Only one family was to be spared, the family of Noah, because he was a truly good man, who thus "found grace in the eyes of the Lord."

Noah was the tenth patriarch, or father of a family, in Adam's race; and he was six hundred years old before the threatened destruction of mankind took place. God warned him that a great flood would visit the earth, and gave him directions how to build a large boat, or ark, in which he and his family could take refuge. This ark was at once begun, as God had commanded, although all Noah's neighbors laughed at him, and paid no heed when he begged them to turn from their wicked ways and repent.

At the end of one hundred and twenty years the ark was finished. In obedience to God's command, Noah then entered into this ship, with his wife, his sons Shem, Ham, and Japheth, and their wives. There were, therefore, eight human beings in the ark, besides the animals which it contained. Of these Noah took with him one pair of every kind that was "unclean," or not fit for sacrifice; but of the "clean" animals he took seven of each kind,—three pairs and an extra male for sacrifice.

So great was the throng of animals which pressed about the ark that it took them seven days to enter it. Then, when they were all safely housed, God shut Noah in. Next he allowed the waters of the deep to rise and overflow, and sent down torrents of rain, which fell for forty days and forty nights.

This great downpour is called the flood, or deluge, and in it perished every living creature that was left upon earth. The waters rose higher and higher, until they overtook and drowned the last fugitives. At the end of forty days, Noah alone remained alive, with his family and the animals which he had taken into the ark. All the wicked people had died, and a new record was about to begin.

The ark, with all its living freight, floated about for five months, before it ran aground upon the peak of Mount Ararat; but two more months passed by before the other mountain tops rose out of the waters.

Forty days later Noah opened the window of the ark, and sent out a raven. The bird flew to and fro, but did not come back to the boat. In the course of the next week Noah sent forth a dove, which flew back; and a few days later he sent it out again and it brought back an olive twig with young leaves.

Noah joyfully received this olive twig, because he knew it was a sign that the waters had gone down, and that even low trees were now entirely uncovered and were putting forth new leaves. Ever since then an olive branch has been considered an emblem of peace and good tidings.

After waiting another week, Noah came out of the ark; and he again set foot on dry ground when he was six hundred and one years old. He was followed by his family, and by all the animals and birds in the ark. Then the first thing that he did was to give thanks to God for saving him. He built an altar upon Mount Ararat, and there offered up a sacrifice of every kind of clean bird and beast.

CHAPTER V

NOAH'S DESCENDANTS

GOD was much pleased by Noah's act of piety in giving thanks and offering a sacrifice as soon as he came out of the ark. For this reason he promised the patriarch that he would never curse the earth again on account of man, nor destroy it. He added that he would be patient with all living things, and would never send such a flood again as long as the earth lasted.

The blessing which had been spoken in the Garden of Eden, "be fruitful and multiply," was repeated; and the animals were again made subject to man, who was now allowed to eat meat for the first time.

Besides the law about the killing of animals for food, God now made a decree against murder, saying that he who "sheddeth man's blood, by man shall his blood be shed." That is why murderers are still put to death.

God then made a covenant, or agreement, with Noah, and said that if men obeyed him he would watch over them and not destroy them; and as a reminder of this promise, he set the rainbow in the clouds. This is the reason why you will often hear the rainbow called the "bow of promise."

Although God had saved Noah and his family, to begin a new race, it soon became plain that they too would sin; for Noah himself yielded to the low vice of drunkenness. His son Ham found him in a drunken sleep, and went and told Noah's other sons, mocking him.

Shem and Japheth were shocked and ashamed, but they did not join in their brother's mockery. Instead of this, they threw a great cloak over their sleeping father, to hide him from their own and everybody else's eyes.

When Noah came to his senses, he was bitterly ashamed; and when he heard how rude Ham had been, Noah sent him away, and cursed him, saying that his children would be slaves. This prophecy came true, and Ham was the ancestor of the black, or negro, race, who were slaves even in this country half a century ago.

Noah then rewarded Shem and Japheth for their dutiful conduct, by blessing them. In time, Japheth's descendants became the ancestors of all the European nations (and thus of the Americans); while Shem was chosen as the father of the race of the Jews. You will often hear it called the "Chosen Race," because God gave his laws to this people, and said that the Messiah would be born among them.

Noah lived three hundred and fifty years after the flood, and died when he was nine hundred and fifty years old. The date of his death is said to be just halfway between the creation of Adam and the birth of Christ, whom the Christians consider as the Redeemer promised when Adam and Eve were driven out of Eden.

Noah died just one year before the great patriarch Abraham was born; but the story of creation passed directly from Adam to Methuselah, from Methuselah to Noah, and from Noah to Terah, the father of Abraham. Thus, although it was not yet written, but only told, it could not have changed much, although so many years had passed since the creation of Adam.

The Bible tells us that the descendants of Noah's sons spread, in the course of time, all over the face of the earth. In a few words it says that Japheth's race included all the Gentiles (people who were not Jews). One of the descendants of Ham was Nimrod, a mighty hunter and king, and the founder of a great city called Babylon. Some of Nimrod's descendants built the city of Nineveh also, and formed the great Assyrian Empire.

The only one of Noah's sons whose story is given at length in the Bible, is Shem, the ancestor of the Jewish race. In his days "the whole earth was of one language, and of one speech," and we are told that the people generally wandered about in search of good pasture for their large flocks, which were their chief possession.

Journeying thus from place to place, Shem's descendants came at last to the plain of Shinar, where Nimrod lived. Here the soil was mostly clay, so the people soon learned to make bricks, and to use them for building houses.

CHAPTER VI

THE TOWER OF BABEL

THERE were plenty of building materials on the plain of Shinar, so the people soon fancied that it would be a fine thing to join Nimrod and found a world-wide empire, with a great city as its capital. Nimrod, it seems, was at the head of this plan, and greatly encouraged them. He hoped that if all the people were banded together, he would be able to prevent them from being scattered all over the face of the world, as God had said he intended to have them.

The work of building was therefore begun, and by Nimrod's orders a huge tower was erected near the new city. But "the Lord came down to see the city and the tower, which the children of men builded;" and it did not please him. To defeat their plans, God confused the tongues of the builders, so that they spoke different languages; and then, as they could no longer understand one another's speech, the men left off working together.

People who do not understand one another are sure to quarrel, and before long the builders went off in different directions, in search of new homes, where they

BUILDING THE TOWER OF BABEL

could speak their own language in peace. Thus Nimrod's plan to found a great empire came to an end, and the Tower of Babel (confusion) was never completed.

Terah, the father of Abraham, was the eighth in direct descent from Shem, son of Noah. Besides Abraham, he had two other sons, Nahor and Haran, who were probably much older than Abraham. The brothers all married, and for some time dwelt in the ancient city of Ur; but before long God called to Abraham, and bade him go into a new land which would be given to him. In obedience to this call, the whole family set out, and made their home east of the Euphrates River, where Terah died when Abraham was seventy-five years old.

Nahor, the oldest living son of Terah, claimed the land where they had settled as his inheritance; and, after a second call from God, Abraham continued his journey, traveling southward with his wife Sarah, and his nephew Lot. They were going in search of the land promised by God, for Abraham fully trusted in these words which the Lord had spoken:

"I will make of thee a great nation, and I will bless thee, and make thy name great, and thou shalt be a blessing; and I will bless them that bless thee, and curse him that curseth thee, and in thee shall all families of the earth be blessed."

These last words, as you see, contained a new promise of a Redeemer, like the one made to Adam, and God now added the information that this Redeemer would bless even the Gentiles,—that is to say, the people who did not belong to the Chosen Race.

Abraham now crossed the Euphrates River, and hence received the name of Hebrew, which is borne by his descendants, and which means "the man who has crossed the river." He passed through the desert, crossed the river Jordan, and entered the Holy Land, where he rested for a while.

From there Abraham wandered on in search of pasture, until he came at last to the rich land of Egypt. Here he was in a strange country, among a strange people. He was afraid they would kill him to obtain possession of Sarah, his wife, so he coaxed her to say that she was only his sister.

The people, thinking that Sarah was an unmarried woman, carried her off to the king's palace to be his wife; but, as soon as she arrived there, a terrible disease visited all the family of the king. At first no one knew the cause of this sickness, but finally the king found out that it had been sent to punish him for trying to take another man's wife.

He had no intention of doing so wicked a thing, so he at once sent Sarah back to her husband, and reproved Abraham for deceiving him. He also bade Abraham leave the country, saying that he did not wish to keep a man who had brought him nothing but harm.

Thus forced to wander on, Abraham traveled northward until he came to Bethel, in the Holy Land, where he had once rested, and where he rebuilt the altar to worship God.

His cattle had now become so numerous that it was very hard indeed to find pasture enough for all his flocks. One day a quarrel arose between the shepherds of Abraham and those of Lot; and, to prevent a renewal of it, the uncle and nephew decided to part. As Lot was the son of an elder brother, Abraham gave him the first choice; and he passed down the valley to the eastward, where the pasture seemed the best. Then Abraham, still trusting in the promises of God, moved a little way towards the south, where he again rested and built another altar.

CHAPTER VII

THE BIRTH OF ISHMAEL

AFTER parting from his uncle, Lot went down into the fertile valley of the lower Jordan, and pitched his tents near the five rich cities of the plain, among which were Sodom and Gomorrah. These cities were ruled by five kings, and in them dwelt men who were as wicked as wicked could be.

Lot, who was a good man, did not enjoy the neighborhood of these wicked people; but, instead of going away, he lingered there until a war broke out between the five cities and a powerful king who claimed tribute from them.

A battle was fought, in which the Kings of Sodom and Gomorrah were killed. Their cities were then robbed; and Lot, being found on their lands, was carried off into captivity with all the rest of the people, and all his possessions were taken away from him.

The news of Lot's peril was brought to Abraham. As soon as he heard it, he hastily gathered together the three hundred and eighteen men of his household, and, accompanied by the Amorites, his friends, he hurried off to rescue his unlucky nephew.

This small troop overtook the victors near the sources of the Jordan. There, by cleverly dividing his forces, and surprising the enemy in the middle of the night, Abraham managed not only to beat them, but to free Lot and to get back all the spoil they had taken.

The little army then came home in triumph, and Abraham gave back the spoil to the new King of Sodom. He kept only the tenth part for the King of Salem, a priest of the Lord, who came to meet him, and gave him bread and wine, and blessed him.

Abraham, having thus saved Lot from the hands of his enemies, went home, where he was soon made happy by a vision from God. This time the Lord repeated all the promises he had already made, and told Abraham that he would have a son. Then pointing upward, God said that Abraham's descendants would be as many as the stars shining in the blue sky above them.

Now the patriarch was over eighty years old, and had already waited many years in vain for the son whom God had promised him, but yet he believed these words. He also listened respectfully while God foretold that the Hebrews would be treated as slaves in a foreign land for four hundred years, but would finally escape, with larger numbers and greater riches, to take possession of the promised land.

Another time, God bade Abraham practice a religious rite called circumcision. This rite was observed by all the Jews after that, and it finally became the mark of the Hebrew nation, just as baptism is the outward sign of a Christian.

Abraham's faith in God's promises was tried by another long period of waiting. His wife Sarah became so sure that God would never give her a son that she finally persuaded her husband to accept Hagar, her servant, as a second wife. It was not at all unusual in those days for a man to have several wives at the same time; and you will soon see that more than one of the patriarchs followed this custom.

Hagar, Abraham's new wife, soon became the mother of a son called Ishmael, whose birth was foretold by an angel. The messenger of God came to Hagar one day, and told her that this child would be "a wild man;" and it is said that he became in time the ancestor of a wandering race which we now call Bedouins, or Arabs.

Fourteen years after the birth of Ishmael, three strangers came to Abraham's tent; and it is supposed that they must have been angels. After they had rested and eaten, these angels told Abraham that Sarah would have a son. The patriarch believed them, for he had not lost faith in God's promise even yet; but Sarah, who was standing behind the door, laughed at them.

The messengers reproved her for doubting their words, and set out with Abraham toward the cities of the plain. On their way, one of these strangers told Abraham that God was weary of the wickedness of the people in Sodom and Gomorrah, and was about to destroy them in punishment for their sins.

Abraham was horrified when he heard this, and he humbly asked whether God would destroy the guilty cities if fifty good persons could be found within them.

When told that fifty good men would save the towns, Abraham inquired whether forty, thirty, twenty, or even ten righteous men would not be enough, and each time the stranger answered, "Yes."

It was so unlikely that even ten righteous men should be found there that Abraham sadly returned to his tent, while his visitors passed on to the city of Sodom, to find out whether the people were really all wicked, and whether they deserved death.

CHAPTER VIII

THE BIRTH OF ISAAC

WHILE Abraham had been pleading with one of the strangers to spare the wicked cities, the two others had gone ahead, and had entered the city of Sodom. Lot, the only good man in the whole place, invited them into his house to spend the night.

But the people of Sodom, hearing that there were strangers at his house, rushed there, and asked that these should be delivered up, so that they might be put to the torture. Lot refused to give up his guests, and began to defend them with all his might.

The Sodomites, however, were so great in number that Lot would not have been able to resist them had not the strangers struck them with sudden blindness. The rude men now groped their way helplessly through the streets, little suspecting that this attempt to injure strangers had settled their own fate.

As Lot was a very good man, and had not sinned, the strangers now bade him leave the city, with his wife and daughters and all that he had. In hopes of saving some of the people from the threatened ruin, Lot lingered there, until the angels led him out with his wife and daughters, bidding them all not to look behind them, but to escape to the mountains lest they should be burned.

Lot and his daughters obeyed, and did not turn their heads when the fire from heaven rained down upon the cities, and destroyed them and their inhabitants. But Lot's wife, prompted by curiosity, disobeyed. In punishment, she was changed into a pillar of salt.

The place once occupied by these flourishing cities is now covered by the waters of the Dead Sea, and the land all around there is very barren, and shows signs of having once been a prey to a raging fire. Near there are great mountains of rock salt, and the waters of the Dead Sea are so briny and bitter that no fish can live in them.

Although Lot had been saved from destruction, he too sinned greatly soon after this, and like Noah gave way to the vice of drunkenness. In punishment for this sin, God made him the ancestor of two wild races, the Ammonites and the Moabites, who took these names from Ammon and Moab, the sons of Lot's two daughters. These two tribes, as you will see later, were destined to cause many sufferings to the Jews.

After staying a long while at his home, where the three strangers had visited him, Abraham again moved toward the southern boundary of the Holy Land, and came to a place called Beersheba. Here lived the Philistines, who were then ruled by a king named Abimelech. Abraham, fearing him, again declared that

Sarah was his sister; so the king thought that he would marry her.

Warned by God in a dream that Sarah was Abraham's wife, Abimelech gave her back to the patriarch, and added many gifts of great value. When Abraham saw how generous the heathen were, he regretted that he had deceived them, and prayed God to bless them. This prayer was soon granted, and the Philistines began to enjoy great prosperity.

It was during Abraham's sojourn at Beersheba that his faith in God's promises was rewarded; for Sarah bore him a son named Isaac. When this child was old enough to be weaned, Sarah saw Ishmael, the son of Hagar, mocking him. In her anger she begged Abraham to send mother and son both away. He was at first unwilling to do so, but God comforted him with the promise that Ishmael would be the ancestor of a mighty nation.

Provided with a scanty supply of food and a skin bottle full of water, Hagar and Ishmael were sent away from Abraham's tent, and wandered out into the desert. Here their provisions soon gave out, and Hagar, seeing no hope of saving the life of her son, left him lying under one of the desert shrubs, and went off a little distance because she could not bear to see him die.

But God had not forgotten his promise. While Hagar was weeping in despair, an angel bade her fear nothing, repeated the promise that her son Ishmael should be the ancestor of a mighty people, and then pointed out a well whence she might draw water to

HAGAR AND ISHMAEL

refresh him. Thus saved from death, Ishmael grew and dwelt in the wilderness, and finally took a wife from the land of Egypt.

CHAPTER IX

ABRAHAM'S SACRIFICE

ABRAHAM had already undergone many trials, and his faith had been tested in many ways; but the greatest test was made when Isaac, his son, was about twenty years of age. God now asked him to offer up this son, upon whom rested all his hopes.

In those days a man had the right of life and death over his wife and children, and human sacrifices were not uncommon. Abraham's conscience, therefore, did not trouble him about killing Isaac in this way; but what almost broke his heart was that he was called upon to give up the dearest thing he had on earth, the son for whom he had waited so long.

In spite of his grief, he nevertheless prepared to obey the command which he had received; and he "took the wood of the burnt offering, and laid it upon Isaac, his son." The young man strode ahead without any fear, while his aged father slowly followed him up the mountain, carrying the fire, and also the knife which was to be used for the sacrifice.

Isaac, who had often gone with his father in such journeys, soon noticed something unusual, and said:

"Behold the fire and the wood; but where is the lamb for a burnt offering?"

His father's heart must have been wrung with anguish at this innocent question; but his faith in God made him strong, and prompted the answer which he now gave to Isaac: "God will provide."

When they came up on the mountain, and the wood had been properly laid upon the altar, Isaac allowed himself to be bound and placed upon it. The last moment had come, and Abraham "took the knife to slay his son."

But an angel of the Lord stopped him, crying: "Abraham, Abraham, lay not thine hand upon the lad, neither do thou anything unto him; for now I know that thou fearest God, seeing thou hast not withheld thy son, thine only son, from me."

Looking up at these welcome words, Abraham saw a ram in the thicket near him, and, as God commanded, he now took it and offered it up in sacrifice instead of his son. The Lord had provided a victim, and the patriarch's heart overflowed with joy as he gave thanks with Isaac beside him.

Then the angel of the Lord spoke again, repeating the promise which had already been made to Abraham about his seed, or descendants: "Because thou hast done this thing, and hast not withheld thy son, thine only son . . . in blessing I will bless thee, and in multiplying I will multiply thy seed as the stars of heaven and as the sand which is upon the seashore; . . . and in thy seed shall all the nations of the earth be blessed, because thou hast obeyed my voice."

The spot where Isaac was thus nearly sacrificed in obedience to God's command, was later the site of the Temple of Jerusalem, of which you will hear much. Abraham now said that it should have for its name the Hebrew words meaning "the Lord will provide." Then he joyfully wended his way down the mountain, with the son who had been given back to him from the dead, and returned to his home at Beersheba.

While he was still living there, Abraham heard of the death of his brother Nahor, who left twelve sons. A few years later Sarah died, when she was one hundred and twenty-seven years old. To bury her, Abraham bought the cave of Machpelah, and thus his first real possession in the promised land was a family tomb.

After Sarah had died, Abraham's chief care seems to have been to find a good wife for Isaac, his son. As he did not wish the young man to marry any of the heathen women around there, he finally bade Eliezer, his faithful steward, journey to Mesopotamia, where his kinsmen still lived, and bring back a wife from there.

When Eliezer reached the country where the sons of Nahor dwelt, he sat down by a well. He was perplexed and did not know how to make a good choice. In his trouble he began to pray with great fervor, and said:

"O Lord God of my master Abraham, I pray thee send me good speed this day, and show kindness unto my master Abraham. Behold, I stand here by the well of water, and the daughters of the men of the city come out to draw water; and let it come to pass that the damsel to whom I shall say, 'Let down thy pitcher, I pray thee, that I may drink;' and she shall say, 'Drink, and I will give thy camels drink also,'—let the same be she that thou hast appointed for thy servant Isaac; and thereby shall I know that thou hast shown kindness unto my master."

CHAPTER X

THE MESS OF POTTAGE

IN answer to this fervent prayer, Eliezer, the servant of Abraham, soon saw the girls come out of the city with their great water jars; and when he asked them for a drink, Rebecca, the granddaughter of Nahor, gave him water and slaked the thirst of his camels also.

Eliezer felt sure that this was the maiden whom God intended for Isaac; so he now made known his errand, and offered her the trinkets which he had brought with him. Rebecca accepted them, and led him to her brother Laban, who gave his consent to the marriage, and on the next day Eliezer bore her away.

Isaac was out in the fields at eventide, when he saw the returning caravan. He went eagerly forward to welcome his unknown bride, and then led her unto Sarah's tent; and for the first time he felt comforted for his mother's loss. Isaac was about forty years of age when he married Rebecca, but Abraham was then still hale and hearty, and shortly after this he married a new wife called Keturah.

Abraham and Keturah had many children, but the father sent them all eastward, after giving them large flocks. He did not wish them to stay near his home, lest they should some day lay claim to the inheritance which was intended for Isaac only.

ELIEZER AND REBECCA

Ten years after Isaac's marriage, Shem, the son of Noah, died, and ten years after that Rebecca bore twin sons, Esau (the hairy) and Jacob (the supplanter). These two boys quarreled even during infancy, and this was the first sign of the enmity that was to exist between the two nations which sprang from them,—the Israelites and the Edomites.

The twin brothers were as different in looks as in character. Esau was rough, hairy, and violent-tempered, and loved the excitement of the chase; but Jacob was handsome, smooth-faced, and gentle, and quietly watched his flocks of sheep.

The brothers were so unlike that it is no wonder they did not love each other; but their natural dislike was increased by their parents, who, instead of treating them alike, had each a favorite. Isaac loved Esau most, because he ate of this son's venison, but Rebecca preferred the gentle Jacob.

The brothers' quarrels, however, were not very serious at first, and Isaac paid no heed to them. His attention was all taken up by his father, Abraham, who fell sick at about this time. Soon after, the old patriarch died at the age of one hundred and seventy-five, and was laid to rest in the cave of Machpelah by his two sons Isaac and Ishmael.

After Abraham's death, Isaac was the head of the Chosen Race, and we read in the Bible that God blessed him.

Isaac's twin sons were about thirty-two years old, when Esau one day came back from the hunt almost famished, and found Jacob with a smoking dish of lentil pottage.

In those days it was not easy to get food at a moment's notice, and Esau was so hungry that he eagerly offered Jacob his birthright, or place as eldest son, in exchange for the pottage. Jacob accepted, and thus, although he was the younger son, he became his father's heir, and could claim as his share the promised blessing that "in his seed all families of the earth should be blessed."

Ever since then, when any one sells anything very precious for a mere trifle, people are apt to say, "He has sold his birthright for a mess of pottage." This is because they remember how Esau gave up the hope of being the ancestor of the promised Redeemer, simply that he might satisfy the cravings of his hunger.

At first Isaac knew nothing of this exchange, but Rebecca was well aware of it. Shortly after the bargain had been made, a famine came, and Isaac was forced to leave home, and to wander southward, into the territory of the Philistines.

He was about to go farther still, and even journey down into Egypt, when God appeared to him, bade him remain where he was, and solemnly renewed all the promises that he had made to Abraham.

While Isaac was dwelling here among the Philistines, he repeated the mistake twice made by his father. When asked who Rebecca was, he replied: "She is my sister." This falsehood was soon found out by the Philistine king, but he nevertheless allowed Isaac to stay in his land.

When the Philistines saw how very prosperous Isaac was, they became jealous of him and said: "Go from us, for thou art much mightier than we." Then, seeing that he did not depart, they tried to drive him away, by claiming in turn each new well that he dug. Isaac was almost in despair, but he finally made a treaty with them, and thus obtained peace.

CHAPTER XI

JACOB'S LADDER

I SAAC was more than one hundred years old, and was nearly blind, when he made up his mind to give his solemn blessing to his heir. This ceremony would make known to all men that this was the son chosen to continue the race which was in time to give birth to the Redeemer.

Isaac intended to give his blessing to Esau, and bade him prepare a venison feast for the occasion. While Esau was away hunting, Rebecca made up her mind to secure the birthright for her favorite Jacob; for she knew that her eldest son had given it up of his own free will.

As she did not dare claim it openly, she tried a fraud. Jacob's smooth hands and arms were covered with hairy goat skin, so that they would seem like his brother's to the touch, and a savory stew was prepared. Isaac, believing that it was Esau whom he touched, then gave to Jacob his solemn blessing before Esau came home from the chase.

Esau, upon entering the tent, found out what had been done, and realized then for the first time how great was his loss. Falling at his father's feet, he cried wildly, "Bless me, even me also, O my father!"

But it was too late. The solemn blessing, once given, could not be recalled. Isaac could not give back to Esau the first place, forfeited by weakness; nor could he make Esau the ancestor of the Messiah. Nevertheless, the father blessed his elder son also, and promised him much worldly prosperity to take the place of the greater blessing which he had lost forever.

ISAAC BLESSING JACOB

Now, although it was all his own fault, Esau could not forgive Jacob for taking his place; and he secretly made up his mind to kill his brother as soon as Isaac had passed away. Rebecca found out these evil intentions; and, to prevent any harm to Jacob, she sent him to visit her brother Laban in Mesopotamia, under the pretext of finding a wife among the daughters of his own race.

Esau was very angry when he heard that Jacob was out of reach, and about to marry in a way that would please his father so greatly. To win back his father's favor, Esau sent away his heathen wives, and married a daughter of Ishmael; but he did not give up all hopes of killing Jacob, and getting back his inheritance.

Jacob, in the mean while, had journeyed on; and when night overtook him he lay down upon the hard ground, with a stone for a pillow. While he was slumbering thus, he had a marvelous dream, and fancied that he saw a great ladder leading from earth to heaven.

On this ladder were "the angels of God ascending and descending," and "the Lord stood above it and said: 'I am the Lord God of Abraham thy father, and the God of Isaac.'" Then God promised that he would give the land to Jacob's descendants, and would be with him and take care of him wherever he went.

When Jacob awoke, he piled up in the form of a rude altar the stones near where he lay. Then he poured oil upon them to consecrate them, and called the spot Bethel (the house of God), before he continued his journey.

Jacob was about seventy years old when he came to Mesopotamia, and sat down near the selfsame well where Eliezer had found his mother, Rebecca. Here Jacob first saw Rachel, Laban's daughter, who invited him into her father's house, where he tarried for a month as a guest.

During this month, Jacob daily saw Rachel, and learned to love her very dearly; and he soon entered into an agreement with Laban whereby he would obtain her hand in marriage at the end of seven years, in exchange for his faithful services as shepherd.

Such was the love which Jacob felt for Rachel that these seven years of servitude "seemed unto him but a few days." As soon as they were ended, however, he went to seek Laban, and eagerly claimed his bride.

Laban prepared for the wedding, but, instead of giving up Rachel, he married Jacob to his eldest daughter, Leah. The bride was so closely veiled during the ceremony that Jacob did not find out the fraud until it was too late. He was very angry indeed at this deception, and refused to be pacified until Laban promised to give him Rachel also; but this was on condition that Jacob should continue to serve his father-in-law for another term of seven years.

As in those days it was quite customary to have several wives at once, Jacob consented, and soon married Rachel. Then, at the request of Rachel and Leah, he also married their handmaidens. During the seven years which followed, Leah and the two servants gave birth to ten sons,—Reuben, Simeon, Levi, Judah, Issachar, Zebulun, Dan, Naphtali, Gad, and Asher. Leah also had a daughter named Dinah; but Rachel, Jacob's favorite wife, had no children at all.

CHAPTER XII

JACOB'S RETURN HOME

AS we have seen, Rachel was the only one of Jacob's wives who had no children. She was much grieved to have no son, because every Jewish woman was anxious to have one, as he might be the Redeemer promised in the Garden of Eden. Rachel mourned greatly, but it was only when the second term of Jacob's servitude was near its end that she became the mother of Joseph.

As this son was the child of his favorite wife, Jacob loved him more than all the others; and, immediately after his birth, the father tried to leave Laban, and become his own master once more. But Laban would not let him go, and promised that if he would only serve for a third term of seven years, he should receive a certain part of the produce of the flocks.

Jacob consented, and during these seven years his herds prospered remarkably well. The time was nearly at an end, when he was favored by a vision, in which he was told to go back to the place where he was born, with his wives, children, and all the wealth that he had won.

As he feared that Laban would again try to detain

him, Jacob got ready in secret, and stole away during the night. Thus, twenty years after he had left his father, he again crossed the desert, and came to the Holy Land.

Laban was very much displeased when he found that Jacob was gone. In his anger he set out to pursue his son-in-law, and soon overtook him. Then he reproached Jacob for going away without taking leave of him, and asked him to give back the household gods, which Rachel had carried off.

Although Laban was at first so angry, he parted peacefully with Jacob, because God warned him not to do his servant any harm. While still on the homeward journey, Jacob had another vision, and saw the angels camping around him, to keep him from all harm.

As he drew near home, his memory of the past grew clearer, and he remembered that he had parted from his brother Esau in anger. He now began to fear that his brother might still wish to kill him, and, hoping to disarm Esau's wrath, he sent a messenger to say that he was coming.

This man soon came back and said that Esau was coming to meet his brother, with an escort of four hundred fighting men. Jacob was terrified when he heard this. In his distress he called to God for help, and then, knowing that a man who wishes aid should exert himself, he got ready to meet the coming danger.

First, he sent a princely present of fine cattle to Esau; and then he placed his caravan so that Rachel and his best-loved child should be in the rear, and thus run less risk in case he was obliged to fight. Thus the caravan slowly passed over the ford of a little river; and Jacob, after seeing the people all cross in safety, staid near the edge of the stream.

Here he met a stranger, who fell upon him and wrestled with him all night. It was only near morning that Jacob found out that his opponent was an angel; for the stranger touched the sinews of one of Jacob's thighs and lamed him for life.

In spite of this bodily injury, Jacob clung fast to the angel, crying: "I will not let thee go, except thou bless me." Thanks to his perseverance, he obtained the blessing he wanted, and the angel told him that he would henceforth be called Israel, or soldier of God.

Limping onward, Jacob soon overtook the caravan. Then, hastening to the head of it, he ran forward to meet his brother, Esau, whose anger he hoped to dispel by falling down upon his face before him, and begging his pardon.

Esau, however, had entirely forgotten his wrath. He put his arms around his brother's neck, kissed him, and proposed that they should always live side by side. Jacob was very glad to be on good terms with Esau once more, but he refused this kind offer, because he knew that their servants would never agree.

This meeting over, Jacob continued his journey, passed over the Jordan, and came to Shechem, where he bought a piece of land. Here he pitched his tents, and built an altar to God, and here his daughter Dinah was carried off by the Shechemites.

Simeon and Levi, two of Jacob's sons, were anxious to punish these men for robbing them of their only sister. In doing so, however, they behaved so cruelly that Jacob was angry with them, and said that they had forfeited their right to inherit the blessing which he had received from his father Isaac.

CHAPTER XIII

JOSEPH'S DREAMS

JACOB did not remain very long at Shechem, but soon passed on to Bethel, where he renewed his covenant with God. While on a journey from this place, his beloved wife Rachel died, after giving birth to a second son, named Benjamin. Rachel was buried near Bethlehem, and over her grave still rises a rude dome, which is called her tomb, and is often visited by Jews, Christians, and Mussulmans.

At the next resting place, Reuben, Jacob's oldest son, forfeited his birthright by doing wrong; and soon afterwards the caravan reached Isaac's encampment. Here they found the patriarch still alive, although he was now one hundred and sixty-five years old; and here Jacob sojourned until his father's death, fifteen years later.

Jacob and Esau buried their father, Isaac, in the cave of Machpelah, where Abraham, Sarah, and Rebecca already lay; and then Esau journeyed away to seek pasture for his flocks. His family is little mentioned in the Bible, but we are told that his descendants were the Edomites, who became the enemies of the Chosen Race.

Jacob went on dwelling in the Land of Canaan, and because he "loved Joseph more than all his children," he was very partial to him. To show his affection, he gave this favorite child a princely robe of many colors.

When Jacob's other sons saw that their father preferred Joseph, they grew angry and envious. These wicked feelings grew worse when Joseph told about two dreams which he had had, and which were as follows:

In the first dream he thought he was in the midst of a harvest field, where he and his brothers were binding grain, and he said that he saw their sheaves bow down and do homage to his, which alone stood boldly upright.

In the second dream, "the sun and the moon and the eleven stars made obeisance" to him.

These dreams were, according to the custom of the time, considered as signs of the future; and they were thought to mean that Joseph would rule over his brothers.

The jealousy of the elder brothers was made still greater by this way of interpreting the dreams; and they began to plot how to get rid of Joseph. They soon had a chance to do what they wished; for, before long, Jacob sent Joseph alone to Shechem, to inquire how his sons and flocks were getting along there.

The brothers recognized Joseph from afar by his bright robe, and hastily consulted together how they might kill him. Reuben alone wished to save Joseph, but he did not dare oppose his brothers openly; so he

JOSEPH'S BROTHERS

now suggested that instead of shedding the lad's blood it would be better to put him into an empty cistern near by.

The wicked brothers agreed, and after taking off Joseph's coat of many colors, they lowered the poor boy into the cistern, whence he could not escape without aid. Then they stained his gay garment with the blood of a kid, and sent it back to Jacob, who thought that his favorite son had been devoured by the wild beasts, and bitterly mourned his loss.

Before Reuben could carry out his kind intentions, and release Joseph from the empty cistern, the other brothers sold him to a caravan of passing merchants for twenty pieces of silver; and when Reuben came back, after a short absence, Joseph was already well on his way to Egypt, where he was to be sold as a slave.

We are told very little about the after lives of the older sons of Jacob, although they married and had many children. The story now follows Joseph into Egypt, where he became the slave of Potiphar, an officer at the king's court. Here Joseph worked so faithfully that he was soon promoted to the office of steward, or overseer of all the slaves of the household.

He had not forgotten his father's teachings during this sojourn in a heathen land, and when Potiphar's wife tempted him to do wrong, he refused to listen to her. This made her so angry that she had him sent to prison, where, in due time, Joseph became the jailer's assistant.

CHAPTER XIV

PHARAOH'S DREAMS

IN the course of his daily work in the prison, Joseph often talked with the captives, and thus he once heard the king's baker tell a strange dream. This man said that as he was passing along with three baskets of freshly baked loaves on his head, the birds of heaven swooped down and ate them up.

As the baker seemed anxious to have an explanation of his dream, Joseph told him that the three baskets stood for three days; and that within this time he would be hanged, and his body left a prey to the birds of the air.

The king's chief cupbearer also related a dream, in which he fancied that he pressed the juice of the grapes from three branches into the king's cup, and gave it to his royal master. Joseph then told him that his dream meant that in three days' time he would be back in the palace; and Joseph begged the cupbearer to urge Pharaoh (as the king was called) to set him free also.

Both these predictions came true. The baker was hanged, and the cupbearer was recalled to the palace, where he entirely forgot Joseph. But two years later the king himself was haunted by a dream which none of the learned men at his court could interpret.

The cupbearer now ventured to suggest that perhaps Joseph could be more fortunate than the wise men, and the king at once sent for him. When Joseph appeared, Pharaoh said that he had seen seven fat cows and seven lean cows rise up out of the river. The lean cows ate up their fat companions, but seemed no larger than before.

This dream was followed by another, in which a stalk of branching Egyptian wheat brought forth seven full ears which were at once consumed by seven empty ears.

When called upon to give an interpretation of these two strange dreams, Joseph said that the seven fat cows and the seven full ears meant seven years of plenty, but the lean cows and the empty ears stood for seven years of drought and famine which would follow the seven years of plenty. During this time all the grain left over from the good harvests would scarcely serve to keep the people alive.

Awed by this explanation of the dreams which had baffled his wisest men, Pharaoh now asked Joseph what he had better do. In answer, the young Hebrew advised the king to appoint a prime minister, who should buy all the surplus grain, during the years of plenty, and store it away for future use; and Pharaoh was so pleased that he gave this office to Joseph.

Raised thus suddenly from the position of a mean slave and prisoner to the very highest rank, Joseph was given full power to carry out the wise plan that he had suggested. All honor was shown him, and he was even married to an Egyptian princess, who became the mother of his two sons, Manasseh and Ephraim.

During the seven years of plenty, Joseph bought all the surplus grain, and stored it away carefully in the large provision houses that were built by his orders in different parts of the kingdom. So, when the years of plenty were over and the famine began, the Egyptians knew no want, thanks to Joseph's wise foresight.

The famine spread not only over Egypt, but also all through Canaan, Syria, and Arabia; and at the end of two years, all the money of the Canaanites and the Egyptians had flowed into the king's treasury. Then, by Joseph's advice, Pharaoh accepted the cattle and lands of his people, in exchange for grain; and thus when the famine was ended, money, cattle, and lands all belonged to him.

Still guided by Joseph, the Egyptian king then divided this land among the people, who in payment were to give him one fifth of the produce. This method made the king very rich indeed, and helped the people not only to live through the time of famine, but also to begin cultivating the soil again as soon as the drought was ended.

Although the Egyptians did not suffer much during the time of famine, the misery in all the countries round about was very great. Jacob heard that grain could be bought in Egypt, so he decided to send ten of his sons thither, in search of food for their families and flocks.

He kept Benjamin at home, for he was afraid that something might happen to him.

The ten brothers started out, with camels and donkeys, and came before Joseph, who at once knew who they were. Seeing that they did not know him, he questioned them with pretended severity, and made believe to consider them as spies. But finally he let nine of them go home with a supply of grain. He kept Simeon a prisoner, however, and said that he would not let him go, or give them any more grain, until they brought their brother Benjamin with them, as proof that the story which they had told was true.

CHAPTER XV

JACOB IN EGYPT

ON their way home with the grain they had bought, Joseph's brothers found out that their money had been put in their sacks with the grain, and they wondered greatly. The food which they brought from Egypt was soon eaten up, for their family was a very large one. As the famine was still raging, they soon saw that they would be obliged to go to Egypt to get some more grain.

They did not dare appear before Joseph without Benjamin, so they begged their old father to let him go with them. Jacob would not let him go at first, but finally he yielded to the brothers' entreaties, and the little caravan again went down into Egypt.

Joseph looked with pleasure upon his little brother, who, of course, did not know him; and then, wishing to find out whether his elder brothers could now be trusted, he made up his mind to try them. By his order the travelers were feasted in his own palace, where he sent all the best dishes to Benjamin, and then the eleven brothers were sent away with full sacks of grain.

They had not gone very far before an Egyptian

officer came riding up in haste, and accused them of stealing one of Joseph's silver cups. Although they indignantly cried that they were not thieves, the officer searched their bags carefully, and found the silver cup in Benjamin's sack, where it had been hidden by Joseph's order.

The officer seized Benjamin to put him in prison, and the elder brothers went back with him to Joseph's court. There they offered to remain in prison in Benjamin's stead, if Joseph would only allow him to go back to Jacob, who, they said, would die of grief if his youngest son did not return.

Touched by their affection for their old father and young brother, and sure that they were sorry for the past, Joseph now made himself known to his brothers. He kissed Benjamin, shedding tears of joy, and freely forgave the ten others when they fell at his feet and begged his pardon. Then he let them go home, giving them many messages for Jacob, who was invited to come down into Egypt, with all his family, and stay there as long as the famine lasted.

When Jacob heard that Joseph was not dead, as he supposed, he was very happy indeed. Then, as God told him in a vision to go down into Egypt, and said that his descendants should be brought up again into the promised land, he set out with all his family.

By this time, Jacob had seventy-five sons and grandsons; for his children were all married and so were some of his grandchildren. The caravan soon reached Egypt, where Joseph tenderly welcomed his old father, and even presented him and five of his sons to the Egyptian king.

Pharaoh received the Israelites (as they were called from Jacob's new name of Israel) very graciously indeed, and gave them the best pasture land in Egypt; and Joseph continued to supply them with all the grain they needed, as long as the famine lasted.

Here in Egypt were spent the last years of Jacob's pilgrimage; for he, like all the patriarchs, said that he was but a pilgrim and a stranger upon earth. Jacob dwelt with his sons in peace and plenty, and he lived long enough to see his family increase greatly.

Feeling that his end was near, he finally called all his sons, gave them his blessing, and spoke a prophecy about what was to happen to their descendants, who, he said, would form twelve tribes bearing their names. Joseph and his two sons, Ephraim and Manasseh, first received a special blessing, and then came the turn of the other sons.

As Reuben, Simeon, and Levi had been deprived of their birthright in punishment for their sins, Judah was selected to receive the chief blessing, and his father told him that the power should remain in the hands of his family until the prophecies came true.

Then, having bidden his sons bury him in the cave of Machpelah, where his ancestors lay, Jacob died when he was one hundred and forty-seven years old. Joseph had his father's body embalmed, after the Egyptian fashion, and then, having obtained Pharaoh's permission, he and his brothers carried it to Machpelah.

When they came back to Egypt, the brothers began to fear that Joseph would avenge himself for his injuries, now that his father was dead. Joseph soon perceived this fear; so he "comforted them, and spake kindly unto them," for he did not owe them a grudge for what they had done.

Joseph lived fifty-four years after his father's death, and saw his children to the fourth generation. Before dying, he gave orders that his body should be embalmed, and carried back to the promised land when the Israelites went back there to live, as God had foretold.

CHAPTER XVI

THE STORY OF JOB

THE grandest Hebrew poem ever written, and the oldest that is preserved, is supposed to belong to this period. You will find it translated in the Bible, where it is called the Book of Job. It tells the story of a chief in the land of Uz, who was very rich.

This man Job is described as a good and honest man, of whom God himself said that he was without his like in all the East. Satan, the tempter, appears again in this poem, and, after visiting all the earth, presents himself before God, who inquires:

"Whence comest thou?"

"From going to and fro in the earth," answers Satan, boldly.

God next asks him whether he has seen Job, and whether he does not admire the man for his great goodness. As Satan would like all men to be as wicked as himself, he answers that Job is good only because he is so prosperous, and that if he were only tried he would soon forget his piety, and even curse his Maker to his face.

To prove the loyalty of his servant Job, God now gives Satan permission to try him in every way, and poor Job suddenly finds himself without wealth or children. But his patience is quite as great as his losses, and although he weeps for his children, he humbly says: "The Lord gave, and the Lord hath taken away; blessed be the name of the Lord."

As Satan has failed in this test, he now gets permission from God to inflict terrible bodily sufferings upon Job, and to make his wife torment him greatly. But, although Job is racked with pain, he merely says: "What! shall we receive good at the hand of God, and shall we not receive evil?"

The second test having also failed, Satan now sends Job's three friends to him, and they talk to him, and insist that he must have committed some great sin, or he would not suffer so much.

These friends go on reasoning with him for many days, and they ask him many questions, all of which he answers very patiently. Indeed, through all their long talk, Job remains so gentle that it is customary even now to describe great patience by saying that a person is "as patient as Job."

After Satan has done his very worst, and has tormented the poor man in every way, God comes to reprove the friends, and to defend Job. God now restores him to health, wealth, and prosperity, giving him seven sons and three daughters, and allowing him to live long enough to see his descendants to the fourth generation.

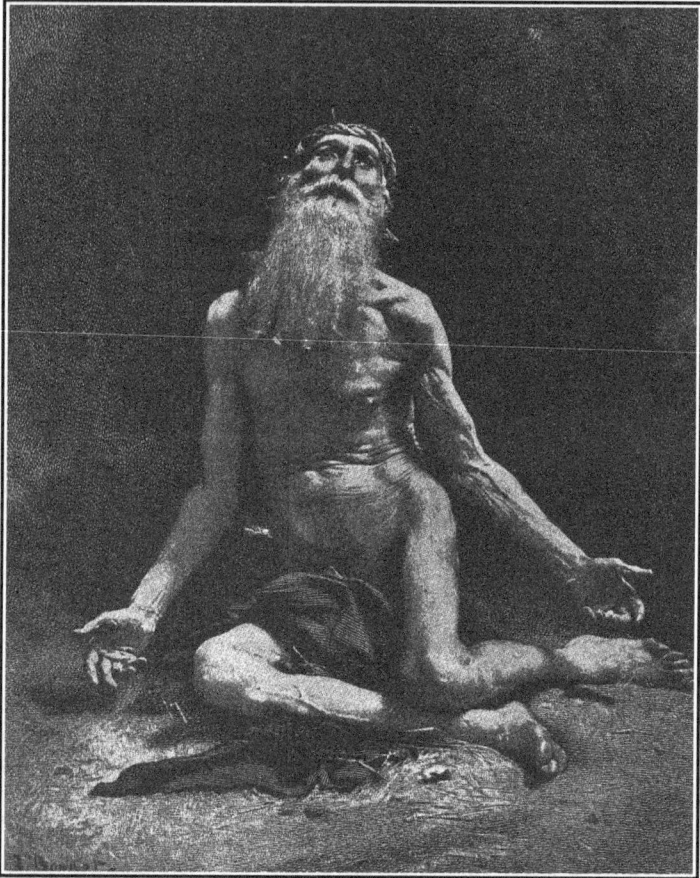

JOB

The story of the Book of Job has been told here because it is probably much older than the Book of Exodus, the second book of the Old Testament. The first book of the Bible ends with the story of Joseph; and in the Book of Exodus you will hear how the descendants of his father Jacob, or Israel, escaped from Egypt after living there about four hundred years.

CHAPTER XVII

THE TEN PLAGUES

A T this time, the Egyptian king, or Pharaoh, was a man who had never seen Joseph, and cared but little for his kinsmen. He was a very stern ruler, and was afraid that the people of Israel would either join his enemies, or leave his land, where they were doing him good service. So he made them his slaves, and had them watched by Egyptian overseers.

The Pharaohs were all great builders, and this one employed the Israelites in making bricks for the erection of two great treasure cities. While they were thus forced to work hard, the Israelites were very unkindly treated; but they had many children, and were steadily increasing in numbers. Pharaoh, seeing this, now gave orders that all their male children should be killed as soon as born.

The nurses who received these orders were God-fearing women, and did not obey them. Then Pharaoh sent his officers to throw all the boy babies into the Nile River.

There was, in those days, a descendant of Levi, who married and had two children,—Miriam and Aaron.

Shortly after Pharaoh had given orders that all the boy babies should perish, a third child was born to this Levite. As this baby was a son, the anxious mother hid him for three months, lest the officers should find and kill him.

At the end of that time the mother felt that she could not keep the babe hidden much longer. So she placed him in a little ark, or cradle, among the reeds by the side of the river, and bade Miriam stand close by to watch over her baby brother.

Soon after, Pharaoh's daughter, the haughty Egyptian princess, came down to the river to bathe. Her glances were caught by the strange object in the bulrushes; and when it was brought to her, and she saw the smiling baby, she said that she would adopt it.

Miriam then stepped forward and offered to find a nurse for the child. Her offer was accepted, and thus the boy Moses grew up in the king's palace under the care of his own mother, who had saved her child to become one of the greatest men the world has ever known.

We know nothing about the early youth and manhood of Moses, but his mother must surely have taught him to honor God. She also told him the story of his adoption, and of the Chosen Race of Israel, to which he belonged.

Moses received an Egyptian education in Pharaoh's palace, where he became "mighty in words and in deeds." He was about forty years of age, when he once saw an Egyptian overseer beating one of the poor Israelites, whose lot had daily grown harder to bear.

In a fit of anger, Moses fell upon the cruel Egyptian, and killed him. No one saw the murder, but the deed was soon found out, and Moses fled into the desert, near the Red Sea. Here he took refuge among the Midianites, who were descendants of Abraham and his last wife, Keturah. While there, Moses saw that some rude shepherds would not allow Jethro's daughters to come near the well to water their sheep. He helped the maidens, and then went home with them and became their father's shepherd. Soon after this Moses married one of these girls, and became the father of two sons.

Moses remained here in the desert forty years, and during that time the Egyptian king died and was followed by another Pharaoh fully as cruel as he. This new ruler oppressed the people of Israel so greatly that they began to pray to be set free; and God, remembering his promises to Abraham, Isaac, and Jacob, prepared to help them.

One day, when Moses was alone with his sheep, he saw a bush near him all wrapped in flames. Strange to relate, however, the dry branches were not burned up; so Moses drew near in wonder to examine the bush.

Suddenly he heard a voice, telling him to take off his shoes, because the ground whereon he stood was holy. Then God spoke to him, gave him a message for Pharaoh, and bade him go and lead the chosen people out of the land of Egypt, and into the desert.

This was a very hard task, and Moses, who had grown old and prudent, was afraid to undertake it. As he did not dare to refuse openly, he began making excuses;

but God now cut these excuses short and bade Moses throw down his rod. As soon as he had done so, God changed the stick into a serpent. Then he restored it to its usual form, and made Moses a leper. God soon cured him of this loathsome disease, however, and promised to perform many miracles to help him.

Moses was encouraged by this promise, and by the permission to have his brother Aaron act as his spokesman, for he himself was slow of speech; so he now undertook to carry out the Lord's commands. Armed only with rods, he and Aaron presented themselves before Pharaoh. There they told the king that the Lord had ordered them to lead the Israelites into the desert, to celebrate a feast.

The King of Egypt, who did not worship God, haughtily asked, "Who is the Lord, that I should obey his voice?" And he said that he would not let the people go.

To force him to obey God's command, Moses raised his wand, and called down, one after another, ten terrible plagues upon the Egyptians. Thus the waters were changed into blood; frogs overran all the land; lice, flies, and sickness tormented man and beast, and all the people suffered tortures from boils.

Then came terrible plagues of hail, locusts, and darkness so intense that people still use the expression "as dark as Egypt." The king, frightened by each new plague, always promised to let the people go as soon as it was removed; but, when all danger was over, he as often broke his promise, and kept the Israelites at work.

Finally, God sent an angel to kill all the firstborn of the Egyptians, and in the darkness of the night this messenger passed from door to door, doing as the Lord had commanded. By Moses' order, all the Israelites had smeared their doorposts with the blood of a lamb; so wherever the angel saw this sign he passed over the house without doing any harm to the people in it.

Pharaoh lost his firstborn too, on this occasion, and now he no longer dared resist, but gave Moses permission to lead the Israelites into the desert.

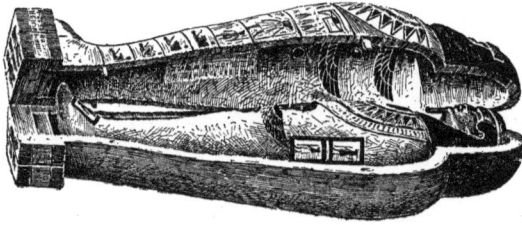

CHAPTER XVIII

THE CROSSING OF THE RED SEA

THE Israelites, having finally got Pharaoh's permission to go out into the wilderness, made ready to start. First they borrowed all the golden ornaments of the Egyptians, and then they roasted and ate the lambs whose blood had marked their doorposts.

When they set out, they carried with them some dough which had not had time to rise; and they baked bread from it at their first halting place. In memory of this flight from Egypt, the Jews, at the yearly celebration of the feast of the Passover, still eat the flesh of a lamb and unleavened bread.

The Israelites numbered more than six hundred thousand men, without counting the women and children; but they all followed Moses into the desert, the Lord himself showing them the way by going before them in a pillar of cloud by day, and in a pillar of fire by night.

The Israelites had not been gone long when Pharaoh regretted having allowed them to depart. So he gave orders that an army should set out in pursuit of them, with "six hundred chosen chariots, and all the chariots of Egypt, and captains over every one of them."

The Egyptian cavalry soon came in sight of the host of fugitives, who had stopped near the shores of the Red Sea. Pharaoh rejoiced, for he imagined that it would now be a very easy matter to force them to turn around and come back.

But the Israelites, who had never been very anxious to leave their homes in Egypt, although they had been so badly treated, were terrified when they saw the sea in front of them, and Pharaoh's army behind them. In their fear, they began to murmur against God, and found fault with Moses for bringing them there only to perish.

But when Moses raised his rod, the waters of the sea parted, and allowed the Israelites to go across dry shod. The waters were held back by a high east wind which God had sent for that purpose, and the gale blew all night, until all the people had passed over.

Morning came, and Pharaoh and his army pursued the fleeing host. But now the wind ceased to blow, and the waters, no longer held back, rushed upon the Egyptians and drowned them all.

The Israelites, who had seen the "great work which the Lord did," now believed the Lord and his servant Moses; and the latter celebrated their deliverance by a grand song of triumph and thanksgiving.

Next Moses led the people southward, into the wilderness, where they suffered greatly from thirst, because they could find no water. At last they came to Marah, where there was water in abundance; but they were greatly disappointed when they found that it was bitter and not fit to drink.

The people began to murmur sorely, but Moses, advised by God, sweetened the water by a miracle, so that they could drink to their hearts' content. From Marah the Israelites now wended their way through the desert once more, until they came to an oasis, where they rested for a while.

When they began their journey again, they passed into another part of the wilderness, where the food which they had brought with them soon gave out. As the Lord did not wish his people to starve to death, he now sent them plenty of quails, and rained down their daily bread from heaven in the form of Manna.

On this occasion God reminded the Israelites that they were to do no work on the Sabbath, for no manna fell then, while a double portion was given them the day before.

By Moses' order a measure of this heavenly food was gathered and carefully kept, so that the Israelites, in years to come, might show their children a sample of the wonderful food upon which they had fed all the time that they were in the desert. Strengthened by this food, they journeyed on in comfort, until they again began to suffer from lack of water.

The ground was hard and dry, and there was not a stream to be found where the people could quench their thirst. They were in despair, and Moses, not knowing what else to do, began to pray for water. In answer to this prayer, God bade him strike a certain rock with his wonderful rod. As soon as Moses had done so, there gushed forth from it a stream of pure water. The people, who saw this miracle with delight, could now satisfy their great thirst, and as they did so they thanked God for giving them plenty of water in time of need.

Danger of death from lack of water was scarcely over, when the Israelites saw the army of the Amalekites coming to meet them. As soon as Moses saw these foes, he bade his captain, Joshua, lead the fighting men against the enemy, while he himself knelt on a hill near by, fervently praying for victory. There he soon noticed that as long as his hands were uplifted his people were strong, but that the Amalekites had the best of the fight as soon as he let his hands fall. So, fearing that his arms might drop from weariness, Moses bade his brother Aaron and another man stand on either side of him, and support his hands, while he fervently prayed until the victory was won.

CHAPTER XIX

THE GOLDEN CALF

SHORTLY after the battle with the Amalekites had been fought, Moses' father-in-law, Jethro, came to the Israelite camp, bringing Moses' wife and sons to him there. He then gave Moses very good advice, and bade him select judges, who would help him to govern his followers.

After parting from Jethro, Moses and his people resumed their journey, and in the third month after their flight from Egypt, they reached the awful wilderness around Mount Sinai. There they lingered at the foot of the mountain, while "Moses went up unto God," and received a solemn promise that if the Israelites would only obey him, he would make of them "a peculiar treasure . . . above all people, . . . a kingdom of priests, and a holy nation."

The elders, in the name of all the people, promised obedience, and after three days of purification "Mount Sinai was altogether on a smoke, because the Lord descended upon it in fire." The people, frightened at this sight, drew back from the mountain in terror, crying, "Let not God speak with us lest we die."

As they were afraid to hear the voice of God themselves, they asked Moses to go up on the mountain, and speak with the Lord. There, on Mount Sinai, Moses received from God the ten commandments, and when he came down he bade the people build an altar, and offered up a solemn sacrifice.

Then, leaving Aaron and another man to govern the people during his absence, Moses went up the mountain once more, where he staid without food for forty days and forty nights. This time he received many directions from God concerning the Tabernacle, or holy tent, and the way in which he wished the people of Israel to worship.

THE TABERNACLE

At the end of the forty days, Moses came down the mountain side, carrying two stone tables, upon which God himself had written the ten commandments that he wished his people to keep.

Moses had just come within sight of the camp,

when he dashed these tables on the ground at his feet; for there, before him, he saw Aaron and the people worshiping a golden calf, which they had made from the spoil they had carried away from the Egyptians.

Moses was very angry when he saw that the people had already disobeyed God's first command. He burned the idol, ground its charred remains to powder, cast this into the water, and made the people drink of it. Then, bidding those who were on the Lord's side come over to him, he made them take their swords and kill three thousand of the Israelites who had worshiped the idol.

After bidding the people purify themselves afresh, Moses again went up the mountain, where, by his entreaties, he obtained God's forgiveness for the erring Israelites. In punishment for their disobedience, God now refused to go before them in person, as he had promised to do if they kept his commands; but he said that he would send his angel instead.

When Moses again came down the mountain, he removed the sacred tent, or tabernacle, to a place outside of the camp. There all the people saw a pillar of cloud descend to its very doors, and heard the Lord speak "unto Moses, face to face, as a man speaketh unto his friend."

After a new journey up the mountain, Moses brought down two new tables of stone, upon which the finger of God had traced the ten commandments. He had been close to God, and the heavenly glory made his face shine so brightly that the people dared not look at him until he drew a veil over his head.

The commandments were again recited in presence of the people, who now brought gifts for the tabernacle; and Aaron and his sons were made priests of God. Then Moses offered up a sacrifice, and God showed his acceptance of it by sending down fire from heaven to consume it.

CHAPTER XX

THE TWELVE SPIES

WHILE the Israelites were stopping at the foot of Mount Sinai, several miracles took place. For instance, two of Aaron's sons dared to put common fire into their censers, in spite of God's command; and they were burned alive by a "fire from the Lord" which fell upon them.

As they had died in punishment for their sin, Moses forbade the people to mourn for them; and because their disobedience had been caused by a moment of drunkenness, he forbade the priests ever to touch any strong drink. Soon after this, a man who took the Lord's name in vain was stoned to death as the new law commanded.

By God's order Moses now counted the grown men, who numbered six hundred and three thousand, five hundred and fifty. This host was divided into four camps, and each tribe had its own captain and place.

The tabernacle was placed in the center of the camp, under the care of the Levites, who were the only priests. Then, when all these arrangements had been finished, Moses again gave the signal for departure, and the

Israelites moved on through the wilderness, under the protection and shadow of a cloud sent by God.

Before they had gone very far, the Israelites began to murmur; and in punishment for this they were burned by a raging fire which swept all through the camp, and never ceased its ravages until Moses won God's pardon for his disobedient people.

Some time later the followers of Moses became weary of manna, and again longed for flesh. So God sent them quails; but instead of eating moderately, they feasted upon them so greedily that they became very sick, and many even died.

During this halt Moses chose seventy elders to help him govern the people; and this council is considered the beginning of the Jewish tribunal called the Sanhedrim, of which you will hear further mention in the New Testament.

In their next stopping place, Miriam and Aaron tried to oppose their brother Moses; for, as they were older, they claimed that their authority was greater than his. Moses was so meek that he did not resist; indeed, his gentleness was so great that it has passed into a proverb, and you will often hear the expression, "as meek as Moses."

Instead of insisting on his right to rule the people, he remained quite still, and God himself took up his defense. Aaron and Miriam were called into the tabernacle, where God rebuked them for their bad behavior, and, to punish Miriam, made her a leper.

This horrible disease was contagious, and Miriam was forced to leave the camp. She was not allowed to return until she was cured by the prayers which Moses made for her recovery.

The long procession of Israelites now wended its way northward, until they came to Kadesh, not very far from the Dead Sea. There twelve men, one from each tribe, were chosen to go ahead and spy out the land which they were approaching, and which God had promised to give them.

These twelve men set out eagerly. They went far up the Jordan River, then came south again, and passed through a rich valley, where grew luxuriant vines. They brought back samples of the produce of the country, and, among other fruits, a bunch of grapes so large that it had to be carried upon a stick between two men.

The spies came back to Kadesh at the end of forty days, and were much pleased by the beauty and fertility of the land, which, as God had said, was "flowing with milk and honey." But although they praised the soil so highly, they alarmed the people by their description of the great walls which were built all around the cities, and by their stories about the size and strength of some of the inhabitants, beside whom they felt like grasshoppers.

The Israelites were frightened by what the spies said, for only one of them, Caleb, refrained from talking about the strength of the inhabitants. Indeed, the people were so discouraged that they began to express their discontent at having traveled so far in vain. Then they broke out into open rebellion against Moses and God, and even proposed to return to Egypt.

Moses and Aaron, in despair, tried to persuade the people that they would triumph if they only believed in God's strength; but it was all in vain. The Israelites murmured until "the glory of the Lord appeared in the tabernacle," and his voice was heard saying that he would disinherit his ungrateful and disobedient children.

At this threat the terrified people were sorry for what they had done, and Moses interceded for them till God relented. He again promised that the Israelites should have the land, but he said that instead of entering it immediately, they would be forced to wander in the wilderness for forty years. He added that none of the rebels should ever be allowed to enter into the land, but that it would be given only to their children.

CHAPTER XXI

THE BRAZEN SERPENT

THE people of Israel were very angry when they heard that their wanderings were to last so long,—so angry that they began to fight the Amalekites and Canaanites, so as to force their way into the promised land. But they soon had cause to repent of this rash behavior, for they were defeated with great slaughter, and driven back into the desert.

Here they wandered about for forty years, fed by the heavenly manna; and, by a merciful miracle, their garments, which they could not replace, did not wear out in all that time.

Very few events are recorded as having happened during those long, weary years; but we find that a man was stoned because he failed to keep the law, and picked up sticks on the Sabbath Day. Another time three men rebelled against Moses and Aaron, and wished to offer up sacrifices on the altar, although God had said that only the sons of Aaron should be his priests.

In punishment for their disobedience, these three men were swallowed up alive by the earth, which opened wide beneath their feet. Then, too, their followers were all burned to death by a fire which came out of the tabernacle.

As the Israelites murmured because these men had been punished for their disobedience, they, too, were called upon to suffer. A frightful plague killed more than fourteen thousand of them, and ceased only when Moses begged God to spare his mistaken people.

To show the Israelites once for all that the house of Aaron was to serve as priests, God now bade the head of each tribe bring his rod, or staff, and lay it upon the altar in the tabernacle. On the next day when Moses entered the holy tent, he found Aaron's rod all covered with buds and blossoms, while the others were only dry sticks as before.

In memory of this miracle, Aaron's rod was placed in the Ark of the Covenant, or sacred chest, which also contained the pot of manna and the stone tables of the law; and this ark, as you will see, was carefully treasured up for many years by the priests who served the Lord.

Terrified into submission by all these signs and wonders, the Israelites gave no more trouble for some time. They walked on and on, and in the fortieth year from the time of the Exodus, or "coming out" of Egypt, they again reached the wilderness near Kadesh.

Thus they had been wandering around the desert in a circle, and now they came back to their former resting place. Here Miriam, the aged sister of Moses, sickened, died, and was duly buried. Here, too, the people who were suffering from thirst murmured again, so God bade Moses speak to the rock and thus procure water.

Instead of doing exactly as he had been told, Moses lifted his rod and struck the rock. The waters gushed forth, but God punished Moses for his impatience by telling him that he would never be allowed to enter the land which had been promised to the Chosen People.

Still advised by God, Moses now led the Israelites to Mount Hor, where Aaron died and was buried. Eleazar, his son, became high priest in his turn, and it was he who now offered up sacrifices for the people.

After mourning thirty days, the Israelites started on again, but they had not gone far when new murmurs were heard. They were punished for this lack of faith by a host of serpents, which bit and poisoned them all. The people died in great numbers, until God, in pity, bade Moses make a brazen serpent, and set it up in the midst of the camp. God then told Moses that he would cure the bites of all those who gazed upon the serpent, thus showing that they wished to be healed.

This brazen serpent was long preserved as a relic by the Israelites. When they forgot the worship of God, they set it up as an idol, and bowed down before it until it was thrown down and broken by order of one of their kings.

We are told that the fragments of the serpent were preserved, and in time passed into the treasury of the Turks. An ambassador from Italy saw them there, four hundred and seventy-one years after the time of Christ, and it is said that he carried them off to the church of St. Ambrose at Milan, where the brazen serpent is still gazed at by travelers from every clime.

CHAPTER XXII

THE DEATH OF MOSES

THE Israelites, delivered from the poisonous serpents, next went through the country east of the Dead Sea, and fought against the people who refused to let them pass. They won a brilliant victory this time, and gained possession of part of the land which was to belong to them. This battle was soon followed by another, in which they defeated the giant king Og, and killed his children and people. The Israelites also won much spoil from him, among other things an iron bedstead thirteen and a half feet long, which they kept as a proof of his great size.

Then the Chosen People encamped in the desert plain of Moab, to the great dismay of Balak, the king of that country. He did not dare attack such powerful enemies openly, so he sent for Balaam, a prophet of the true God, and promised him a large sum of money if he would only curse the people of Israel.

Balaam, tempted by the offered reward, consented, but God spoke to him and said: "Thou shalt not go with them; thou shalt not curse the people; for they are blessed." But in spite of this warning, Balaam was so anxious to get the money promised him that he set out with Balak, intending to curse the Israelites, although God warned him to do only as he was told. On the way to the heights upon which he was to stand while speaking this curse, the ass which Balaam rode shied twice, and each time saved him from the sword of an angel. But Balaam did not see why the ass stopped in a gateway, and he beat the poor animal until it turned and spoke to him. At the same moment God opened Balaam's eyes, so that he saw the angel with the sharp sword.

Balaam was so frightened then that he would gladly have gone home, but the messenger of God told him to go on, warning him, however, to speak no words except those which the Lord would put into his mouth.

Balak and Balaam went up three hills, one after another, and three times Balaam opened his mouth to speak the desired curse. But each time God changed the words of this curse into a blessing, because he was watching over the people of Israel, whom he still loved in spite of all their sins.

Then, still speaking as God wished, Balaam foretold the coming of the promised Messiah, or king, and the victories and conquests of the Israelites. Although he had thus been forced, against his will, to foretell the greatness of the Israelites, and although he knew that God was with his people, Balaam soon made a second attempt to harm them, by tempting the men to disobey God's orders, and to take wives from among the Moabites.

To punish the people for this disobedience, God sent another terrible plague, which carried off twenty-four thousand Israelites. Indeed, it did not stop raging until Moses made a law whereby all those who disobeyed were punished by immediate death.

By God's order, Moses now took a second census of the men of Israel. In spite of all the sufferings they had endured in the wilderness, he found that they numbered only eighteen hundred and twenty less than when they left the land of Egypt forty years before.

Joshua was now chosen and publicly named as the successor of Moses; and the tribes of Reuben and Gad received the land which had just been conquered. Before it was given to them, however, they had to promise that their best warriors should march at the head of the Israelite army until all the land was won.

The work of Moses was finished. He therefore bade the people come together to receive his last blessing and made them a solemn farewell speech. In it he reminded them of all that God had done for them in the wilderness. He repeated the prophecies about their future, and the law, and then broke out into a grand song of thanksgiving.

Moses next blessed the awed and waiting people, and then, having received his last summons, he went up Mount Nebo, from whose top God pointed out to him the land promised to his people.

It was here, on the lonely mountain top, that Moses, the servant of God, died; and we are told that God himself laid his body to rest. No one ever knew the place where Moses was buried, but the people mourned him for thirty days before they thought of making their way into the beautiful land which he had seen, although he was never allowed to enter it.

CHAPTER XXIII

THE WALLS OF JERICHO

MOSES, the great lawgiver of Israel, was succeeded by Joshua, the great captain, whose mission it was to conquer the promised land for God's people.

Joshua was already eighty years of age, but he had shown his skill as captain in the beginning of his career by winning a victory over the Amalekites, and lately by conquering the land east of the Jordan. As he had always obeyed, and had never murmured, and as he had been faithful when all the rest were faithless, he was allowed to enter the promised land, and was well fitted to be the leader of the people.

As soon as the thirty days of mourning for Moses were ended, God appeared to Joshua, and bade him lead the people over the Jordan, into the land where spies had already been sent to see how the land lay. These scouts went to the walled city of Jericho, and entered the house of a woman named Rahab. Their strange looks excited the suspicions of the people, who hastily closed the gates of the city so that they could not escape, and began to search for them in order to put them to death.

But Rahab hid the spies so cleverly that no one could find them, and sent the pursuers off on a false track. When they had gone, and all danger was over, she lowered the Israelites in a basket from one of the windows of her house, which was built in the thick walls of the city.

The spies were so grateful to Rahab for helping them that they promised to save her life in their turn. They bade her tie a scarlet thread to the window of her house, so that they would be sure to recognize it; and they promised that the persons in it should escape from all harm when the Lord gave the city into their hands.

By a roundabout way the spies then went back to camp, and made their report to Joshua. Early the next morning, the priests, carrying the Ark, went down to the banks of the Jordan, whose tide was much swollen at this season by the melting of the mountain snows. But as the Levites reached the water's edge, the river divided; "the waters which came down from above stood and rose up," while the remainder flowed down to the Dead Sea. Thus a wide channel was left bare, and the people could pass over dry shod.

By Joshua's command, the priests halted in the middle of the river until all the people had passed over. He also gave orders that twelve men, one from each tribe, should take stones from the river bed with which to build an altar. Then the priests also left the river bed, and the waters, no longer stopped in their course, again rushed downward to the Dead Sea. The army marched on to Gilgal, where the Israelites erected the altar of

RAHAB LOWERING THE SPIES

twelve stones, and celebrated the first Passover in the land which had been promised to them, forty years after their fathers had kept it before leaving Egypt.

Here all the people were circumcised, a religious ceremony which had been omitted during their desert wanderings. Here, too, the supply of manna ceased, and the people baked bread from the grain of the land which was soon to belong to them.

While Joshua was planning how to take the strong city of Jericho, an angel of the Lord appeared to him, and bade him march around the city once a day for six days, with all his host, and seven priests blowing the seven sacred trumpets as they marched before the Ark. The seventh day the army was to march around the city seven times; and when the last circuit was made, they were to blow a loud blast on the trumpets and to raise a sudden shout, at the sound of which the Lord would make the walls fall down flat.

All these directions were carried out with great care. The Israelites marched around the city daily, and when the seventh round had been finished on the seventh and last day, a mighty shout rent the air, and the strong walls of Jericho tottered and fell, as God had promised.

All the people, except Rahab and those whom she sheltered in her house, were killed; their property was destroyed, and the city razed, and Joshua pronounced a solemn curse upon any one who should attempt to rebuild it.

In reward for the good turn she had done the spies, Rahab was given in marriage to an Israelite. In time she became the mother of Boaz, the great-grandfather of David, a well-known king of the Israelites, or, as they are also called, the Jews.

CHAPTER XXIV

THE CONQUEST OF THE PROMISED LAND

GOD had ordered that all the property of the inhabitants of Jericho should be destroyed. Only one man dared transgress this command, by keeping back a small portion of the spoil. He hid it, and fancied that his disobedience would remain unknown and unpunished. But when the Israelites next tried to take a city, they were defeated. Joshua knew that this misfortune would never have happened if the people had obeyed God's commands; so he now fervently prayed that the sinner might be revealed.

Lots were drawn, first among the twelve tribes, then among the divisions of the tribe on which the first lot had fallen, and lastly among the families. By this means the sinner was discovered. He confessed having saved two hundred shekels, or pieces of silver, and was punished by being stoned to death with all his family.

This signal example having been made, Joshua again led the people against the city, which they succeeded in taking by stratagem. Thus the Israelites won all the passes from the valley of the Jordan; and, marching on to Shechem, they erected an altar upon which they inscribed the law.

While the Chosen People were tarrying at Shechem, the neighboring nations made a league against them; but the Gibeonites pretended to be friendly with them. Hoping to make the Israelites believe that they lived very far away, the Gibeonites came in tattered garments and worn foot gear, and brought no provisions but moldy bread.

Without consulting God, the Israelites now made an alliance with them; but when they found out the fraud three days later, they marched against Gibeon, and made all the people their slaves.

Shortly after this, Joshua's troops were attacked by the combined forces of five allied kings, and he would have been overwhelmed by their numbers had he not been helped by a violent hailstorm. Such was the fury of the storm, that there "were more which died with hailstones than they whom the children of Israel slew with the sword."

Joshua began to pursue the fugitives, and seeing that daylight would fail him before the victory was really assured, he commanded: "Sun, stand thou still upon Gibeon; and thou, moon, in the valley of Ajalon." In obedience to this order both sun and moon stood still until Joshua had won a great victory.

Joshua pursued the people to a place where the five kings, his enemies, were hiding in a cave. These monarchs were dragged from their retreat and led away and hanged, just as the sun at last went down and closed the longest day which has ever been known.

By a few more battles Joshua became master of all the southern half of the country, and now he prepared to march northward, and subdue another king, who had an army "as the sand that is upon the seashore in multitude." In spite of this array of warriors, Joshua defeated the king, burned his principal city, put the inhabitants to death, seized their property, and then took possession of all the northern part of the promised land.

Although Joshua had thus conquered all the promised land, many of his enemies were not entirely subdued, and the Canaanites and Philistines still owned much territory. The conquest of their land, however, was reserved for another leader; for Joshua was now very weary and old, and he felt that his end was near.

He therefore called the heads of the remaining ten tribes to him, and portioned out by lot the land which he had conquered. The city of Hebron, however, was given as a reward to Caleb, a man who had never murmured, and who was now the only one left of the twelve spies that had visited the Holy Land forty years before.

The only tribe which received no province at all was that of Levi, because the Levites were chosen to serve the Lord. They were to receive a certain amount from all the people, and the Lord himself "was their inheritance."

Peace now reigned everywhere, and the two tribes

of Reuben and Gad, which had received their portions long before, prepared to recross the Jordan, and go home. As soon as they reached the other side of the river, they began to build an altar. Their brethren, fearing that they were about to forget God and worship idols, immediately sent Phinehas, the son of the high priest, to inquire what it meant.

This messenger soon came back, and the people were greatly relieved when they heard that the new altar was not for the worship of foreign gods. The men had built it merely to remind their children that they too belonged to the Chosen Race, although they were separated from the rest of it by the Jordan's rushing tide.

When all these matters had been satisfactorily settled, Joshua called the heads of the people together, and exhorted them "to keep and to do all that is written in the book of the law of Moses." He prophesied that, if they dared serve other gods, they would lose the land which their God had given them.

Then, after receiving a solemn promise from all the people to remain faithful, and after writing the history of his time, Joshua died peacefully, at the age of one hundred and ten. He was buried in the country which he had won for Israel, a country which is called the Promised Land, the Holy Land, or Palestine.

CHAPTER XXV

THE DEATH OF SISERA

JOSHUA'S death was soon followed by that of the high priest Eleazar, who was succeeded by his son Phinehas. It was at this time, also, that Joseph's remains, so carefully brought from the land of Egypt, were buried at Shechem.

Now all the people went on serving God faithfully as long as the elders lived. This period lasted about forty years, at the end of which time there arose another generation who "knew not the Lord, nor yet the works which he had done for Israel;" so the people of the Lord forgot him, and began to worship the heathen gods.

In punishment for their idolatry, they were given over into the hands of the people whose gods they served, and were forced to endure much ill treatment.

But, although punished, they were not utterly forsaken; for, whenever it was necessary, God always provided judges, who freed them from their oppressors.

No sooner were the Israelites free again, however, than they would return to their old sins, worship false gods, and refuse to obey the law. It was because of this oft-renewed unfaithfulness that God delayed the full accomplishment of his promise to drive all the heathen nations out of the country. The story of these troublous times is written in the Book of Judges, which begins with an account of the efforts made by the tribes of Judah and Simeon to drive out the Canaanites and the Perizzites.

The two tribes of Israelites won a victory and captured the tyrant who ruled over their enemies. This was a man who openly boasted of having cut off the thumbs and great toes of seventy kings, and of having amused himself in watching their vain efforts to pick up the crumbs that fell from his table. In punishment for such deeds of cruelty, the Israelites treated him in the same way, and then killed him in the city of Jerusalem.

Many other attempts to drive the heathen out of the land are recorded in the Book of Judges; but none of them were entirely successful. Indeed, it was not long before the Israelites, in punishment for their sins, were allowed to fall into the hands of the King of Mesopotamia. They suffered under his tyranny eight years, before the Lord heard their cries of distress, and sent them a deliverer in the person of Othniel, a nephew of Caleb.

Othniel ruled the people wisely, and died forty years after Joshua. But as soon as he was gone, the Israelites again fell into idolatry, and because they did so, they were conquered by the Moabites and Amalekites, their old foes, who tyrannized over them for eighteen years.

When their woes had become unendurable, another deliverer arose—Ehud, who was a left-handed man. This fact proved fatal to the Moabites, for Ehud killed their king with his left hand while delivering a pretended written message with his right.

This murder was not discovered till Ehud had escaped. He at once rallied the Children of Israel around him, led them on to battle, and completely routed the Moabites.

Shamgar, the next judge, delivered the Israelites from the hands of the Philistines, and showed his unusual strength by killing six hundred of his foes with an ordinary oxgoad.

As the people had fallen back into idolatry, they were next given over to the cruel treatment of the King of the Canaanites, who allowed his captain, Sisera, to oppress the land for twenty years. At the end of that time, the Lord sent a woman named Deborah to the rescue of his people. This Deborah was a prophetess, and as she herself could not go forth and fight, she sent Barak, the fourth judge, against the enemy.

The two armies met, and once more the Israelites won a great victory. They owed this victory in part to a great storm, which injured the troops of Sisera only. Terrified by the fury of the elements leagued against them, Sisera's soldiers fled, but they were soon overtaken and killed by the Israelites.

Sisera, the captain, escaped alone and on foot, and finally took refuge in the tent of a woman named Jael. There he was given a drink of milk, and after telling the woman to keep his hiding place secret, he lay down and went to sleep.

While he thus thought himself safe, Jael armed herself with a tent pin and a hammer, crept up close to her sleeping guest, and with one terrible blow drove the pin right through his temples and deep into the ground. Then she ran to meet the pursuing host, and, leading Barak into her tent, showed him what she had done. The Israelites had again won the victory, and the history of this epoch closes with Deborah's song of triumph, in which she relates how Sisera was defeated and slain.

CHAPTER XXVI

RUTH AND NAOMI

WE are told that not very long after the death of Sisera, an Israelite named Micah stole eleven hundred shekels of silver from his mother. She, little suspecting that the thief was her own son, cursed the robber, and solemnly vowed to make a molten and a graven image, should she ever recover her property.

Oppressed by remorse for his guilt, Micah finally confessed his theft. He gave back the silver, and helped his mother set up the images in his house, where one of his sons acted as priest.

Still, as the priesthood had been strictly confined to the family of Levi, Micah was not satisfied with this arrangement. He knew no rest until he had secured the services of a young Levite, who, for a certain hire, promised to serve as priest to the images, although he knew that it was against the law.

Five spies from the tribe of Dan paused at Micah's house, when on their way to Laish, and there consulted the Levite. As he predicted that they would be successful, the Danites rewarded him by taking him and the images with them to Laish. They soon became masters of that city, and changed its name to Dan; and then the Levite was established there as their priest.

Another episode belonging to this epoch, is the story of a Levite, who, deserted by his wife, followed her to her father's house, and prevailed upon her to return to him. They set out upon their homeward journey late in the day, and were forced to spend the night at Gibeah, where an old man entertained them hospitably in his own house.

Now the people of Gibeah belonged to the tribe of Benjamin, but they had grown as wicked as the Sodomites of old. They no sooner heard that there were helpless strangers in the city, than they attacked the house and forced the old man to give up the woman. Then they ill-treated her so shamefully that, when morning came, the Levite found her dead on the doorstep.

This crime roused her husband's wrath to such an extent that he cut her body into twelve pieces, and sent them to the twelve tribes of Israel, with a full account of the wrongs he had suffered at the hands of the Benjamites.

The result was a general uprising of the people, who sallied forth four hundred thousand strong, and killed nearly all the Benjamites. Only a few among them managed to escape to the mountains, whence they returned, in time, to their old homes.

Here they married the maidens taken from a city which was destroyed; but as these were not enough to supply wives for them all, they got two hundred more by kidnaping the maids of Shiloh when they came out of their city to dance at one of the great national festivals.

The story of Ruth, which is told at length in the book bearing her name, is one of the most beautiful episodes of this age. It seems that a certain man of Bethlehem was driven by famine into the land of Moab, with his wife, Naomi, and his two young sons.

While in the land of the Moabites, these young men married two native women, Orpah and Ruth, and here father and sons died, leaving three widows to mourn their early death. Naomi was very poor, and in her grief she prepared to return to her own country and people.

When her daughters-in-law heard of this plan, they both offered to go with her, so that she need not make the journey alone. They all three started out on foot, but they had not gone very far when Naomi urged both young widows to go back to their father's house, where they would, in time, forget their sorrow, and even marry again.

Orpah listened to this advice, and after taking a tearful leave of Naomi, she slowly went home. But Ruth clung to her mother-in-law, crying: "Thy people shall be my people, and thy God my God. Where thou diest will I die, and there will I be buried."

As Ruth would not leave her, Naomi now took her to Bethlehem, her old home; and the two widows came there at the time of the barley harvest. They had no money wherewith to buy food, so Ruth, who was young and strong, went out into the country to glean; that is

RUTH

to say, to pick up the stray ears of grain which fell from the full sheaves.

She soon came to the harvest fields of Boaz, a rich kinsman of her father-in-law; and when this man saw the poor young woman's efforts to secure some grain, he kindly bade the reapers drop a few handfuls, so that she might have something to eat.

CHAPTER XXVII

GIDEON'S FLEECE

RUTH gleaned all day in the harvest field, and when evening came she went joyfully home to show Naomi how much grain she had gathered, thanks to the kindness of that charitable man, Boaz.

When Naomi heard this name she started, and at once told her daughter-in-law of his relationship to them. Ruth worked at gleaning every day, and at the end of the harvest time she was greatly surprised when Naomi bade her go back to the field, enter the booth where Boaz and his workmen slept, and lie down at his feet. When he awoke, she was to remind him of the law which commanded that a widow was bound to marry her husband's nearest kinsman, whose duty it was to take care of her.

Although this custom seemed very strange to a Moabite woman, Ruth immediately obeyed. When Boaz awoke and asked her what she was doing there, she told him that she was the widow of his relative, and asked that he should give her her rights.

Boaz then sent Ruth away with a promise that he would do justice to her, although there was a man more nearly related than he. Early the next day, he found out that this man was willing to give up all claim to the young widow; and then he publicly took Ruth to wife.

Thus freed from want, Ruth soon grew happy in her new home; and she became the mother of a son named Obed, the grandfather of David, a great king of whom you will hear much. But Ruth, the Moabite woman, was not the only one of David's ancestors that was not an Israelite; for Boaz, as you will remember, was the son of Rahab, who was spared from the general massacre when the Chosen People took Jericho.

The Israelites, in the mean while, had again misused the peace they had won, and soon after the death of Deborah and Barak, they again began to worship idols. In punishment for this sin, they were now allowed to fall into the hands of the Midianites and the Amalekites, who came in great numbers, being "as grasshoppers for multitude."

The enemy took possession of the land, and drove the Israelites to the caves and dens in the mountain side. Whenever the people of God came down into the valley, they were illtreated and oppressed; and only at the end of seven years did the Lord consider that they had been punished enough, and prepare to deliver them.

The judge sent to save them this time was Gideon, a "mighty man of valor." He was secretly threshing wheat near his father's barn, to save it from the Midianite thieves, when an angel of the Lord suddenly appeared before him, and bade him rescue Israel from the hands of the enemy.

Gideon at first tried to excuse himself, saying that he was neither worthy of such an honor, nor capable of winning it; but the angel repeated the command, and the man, seeing that he was talking to an angel, now wished to offer up a sacrifice to him.

The angel, however, refused this act of worship, which was due to God only, and bade Gideon lay the victim on a rock. When all was ready, the angel touched the rude altar with his staff, miraculously setting fire to the victim, and then disappeared.

Gideon knew that the spot had been made holy by the presence of a divine messenger, so he set up an altar there. That selfsame night, the Lord visited Gideon in a dream, and bade him overthrow the altar of the heathen god Baal, where the people had worshiped, cut down the sacred grove, and offer up his father's bullock in sacrifice to the true God.

When he awoke, Gideon did as the Lord had commanded, and called all the people together. While waiting for their coming, the young leader prayed God to show by a sign that he would save Israel. For this purpose, Gideon spread out a fleece upon the threshing floor, and asked that it should be wet with dew, while the ground all around it staid dry.

When Gideon came on the morrow, he found the fleece so wet that he could wring a great deal of water out of it, while the ground all around it was perfectly dry. But he was not quite satisfied with this one miracle, so he now prayed that the fleece might remain dry and the ground be wet.

This second sign was granted also, and when Gideon saw the dry fleece and wet ground, he believed all that the Lord had told him, and with a force of Israelites, numbering thirty-two thousand men, he marched off to meet and overwhelm the enemy.

CHAPTER XXVIII

DEFEAT OF THE MIDIANITES

GIDEON, as we have seen, had a very large army. But all his men were not needed on this occasion; for it seems that the Lord wished to prove to his Chosen People that they needed only to rely upon him and all would be well.

God therefore spoke to Gideon, and in obedience to his command the general made a proclamation, saying, "Whosoever is fearful and afraid, let him return." Twenty-two thousand men gladly seized the opportunity thus given to leave the army, and hastened away to a place of safety.

Then, seeing that the army was still too large, God bade Gideon lead his men down to the river to drink, and select from among them all those who lapped the water. When counted, these were found to number three hundred men. They were to be Gideon's only army, and with this handful of men he was to drive away all the Midianites.

That same night God bade Gideon go alone with his servant and reconnoiter the enemy's camp. Under cover of the darkness, Gideon and his attendant drew near the camp unseen. There, crouching out of sight, they overheard a soldier relating a dream that he had just had. This man said that he had dreamed that a barley cake had come rolling into their camp, with such force that it had overthrown a Midianite tent.

One of the soldier's companions then began to interpret this dream, and said that the barley cake stood for the sword of Gideon, and that it was plain that the Midianites would be conquered. Gideon, seeing that these soldiers were already a prey to superstitious fears, now hastened back to his own camp, and roused his men. He divided them into three companies, armed them with trumpets and empty pitchers containing lighted lamps, and bade them noiselessly follow him and imitate his every movement.

Silently he now went back to the Midianite camp, followed by all his men, and a little before midnight he gave the signal for attack. At the same moment he and all his men blew their trumpets and broke their pitchers.

The sudden din, the crash, and the blinding light so terrified the Midianites that they all "cried and fled," and in their panic they even fell upon each other with drawn swords.

The Israelites, urged by Gideon, now pursued the fugitives, and slew many of them; but when they came to the towns of Succoth and Penuel, they vainly tried to obtain food. As this was refused to them because the people feared to incur the anger of the Midianites, Gideon cursed the inhabitants of both cities.

He could not pause, however, and rushed on after the fugitives. But when all pursuit was ended, and the Israelite army returned in triumph, Gideon ordered that the men of Succoth should be beaten and the tower of Penuel pulled down. Next, he killed the princes who had refused to help him by giving him food.

In their joy over the successes they had won, the Israelites now came to Gideon and asked him to be their king; but he refused the honor, saying, "The Lord shall rule over you." He did this because he knew that the government of the Chosen People was to be what is called a Theocracy; that is to say, a government in which God is the ruler.

The only reward which Gideon would accept for his services was the golden earrings worn by the slain Midianites. These were collected for him, and amounted to the value of seventeen hundred shekels of gold.

With this precious metal, and the ornaments taken from the king's camels, Gideon made an Ephod, a rich garment for the priest; and it was not long before the ignorant people began to worship this, forgetting the commandment which they had first heard from Mount Sinai in the days of Moses.

Gideon, the fifth judge of Israel, ruled forty years, and during all that time the Midianites did not dare renew their oppression. But when he died, at a good old age, the people again went back to the worship of Baal, and entirely forgot the Lord who had delivered them so many times from the hands of their enemies.

CHAPTER XXIX

JEPHTHAH'S DAUGHTER

ALTHOUGH Gideon had refused the royal power, it was claimed after his death by Abimelech, one of his sons. This young man secured the help of the Shechemites, and, to prevent any one from disputing his claim to the throne, he killed seventy of his relatives.

A prophet was sent to reprove the Shechemites for helping Abimelech, and he did so by telling them a parable, or lesson taught by a story, which is probably the oldest in the world.

He told them that the trees once decided to elect a king, and chose the olive; but the olive tree refused to leave its fatness, to serve other trees. The fig tree, which was next chosen, refused to give up its sweetness, and the vine, its power to cheer; and all the trees and shrubs found some good excuse to decline the honor of being king.

At last the charge was accepted by the worthless bramble, which said: "If in truth ye anoint me king over you, then come and put your trust in my shadow, and if not, let fire come out of the bramble and devour the cedars of Lebanon."

You see, all the other trees were good for something, and had something to live for and to do; but the worthless bramble, which could produce nothing and was only fit for the fire, was ready enough to accept the crown, although it could not even furnish shadow enough to protect any one, and knew that the other trees would suffer if they came near it, and would perish in the fire to which it was condemned.

The prophecy contained in this parable was fulfilled three years later; for Abimelech,—the worthless bramble,—having grown angry with his former friends the Shechemites, came against them with an army, defeated them, and set fire to one of their principal towers, where many people had taken refuge.

He next passed on to Thebez, where he again tried to set fire to the walls with his own hand. But while he was thus occupied, a woman threw a fragment of a millstone down upon his head, and broke his skull. Abimelech did not die right away, but had just time to call his armor-bearer, and bid the man kill him, so that it might never be said that a woman had slain him.

This Abimelech is reckoned as the sixth judge of Israel, although he never did any good to the people, and thereby differed greatly from the judges who came before and after him.

We are told that the civil wars ended with the death of Abimelech, and that the two succeeding judges ruled peacefully over the Israelites. But, as usual, the people soon took advantage of this prosperity to relapse into idolatry, and, as usual, they suffered for this sin by falling into the hands of their enemies.

This time they were conquered by the Philistines and the Ammonites, who tormented them for eighteen years. But when the Israelites had suffered enough, and were thoroughly humbled, God took compassion upon them, and sent Jephthah, the ninth judge, to lead their armies against the foe.

Anxious to obtain a glorious victory, Jephthah made a rash vow, promising to offer up in sacrifice "whatsoever cometh forth of the doors of my house to meet me, when I return in peace from the children of Ammon."

Thanks to the help of God, who delivered the enemies into his hands, Jephthah won a grand victory, secured twenty towns, and so terrified the Ammonites that they did not dare rise up again until long after, in the days of Saul.

Jephthah now returned to his house, but all his joy was turned to sorrow when he saw his daughter come forth to welcome him. Then only did he remember his rash vow, and realize that he would be obliged to give up his beloved child.

When the girl heard of her father's vow, she made no resistance, and only asked that she might have two months' grace. At the end of two months, she came down from the mountains of Gilead, where she had mourned with her companions. Whether her father really made a human sacrifice, which was not unheard of at that day, or whether he merely shut the maiden up in a sort of a convent, where she would spend all her time in prayer, remains a mystery to this day; for we are only told that he "did with her according to his vow which he had vowed."

CHAPTER XXX

SAMSON'S RIDDLE

WHEN Jephthah went forth to fight the Ammonites, he did not ask any help from the Ephraimites. They resented this oversight bitterly, and behaved so insolently that the followers of Jephthah made war against them, and defeated them in a pitched battle.

When the fight was won, Jephthah was afraid that some of the Ephraimites might cross the Jordan, and, returning home, give a wrong impression of the quarrel and stir up their whole tribe to war; so he and his followers decided not to let a man of the conquered army escape.

To make sure of this, they placed a guard at all the fords of the Jordan, with orders to make every man who wished to cross pronounce the word "shibboleth;" for the Ephraimites could not pronounce this word.

After judging Israel six years, Jephthah died in Gilead, where he was buried. He was succeeded by three judges in turn, after whose rule the disobedient Israelites fell into the hands of the Philistines. This time their bondage lasted forty years, and Samson, who lived during the first half of this period, has been called the thirteenth judge of Israel.

Born in the days when Eli was high priest, Samson was the son of a Danite. Before his birth, an angel had appeared to his mother, telling her that she would have a son, who was to be dedicated to God by a special vow, and hence called a Nazarite.

The woman was so amazed at this prophecy that she called her husband, and the angel repeated it to him before vanishing. The child Samson was born as the angel had foretold, and his mother duly dedicated him to the service of the Lord, and never cut off his long hair, which was the outward sign of a Nazarite.

All the tribes of Israel were now under Philistine oppression, and when Samson became a man, the spirit of God began to move him, and revealed itself principally in the matchless strength and courage with which he was endowed.

As this strength all depended on the keeping of his vow to be a Nazarite, the Bible tells us that Samson's strength was in his hair. The young man, conscious of his unusual power, was very brave indeed, and tried hard to provoke a quarrel with the oppressors.

With this purpose in view, he once asked for the hand of a certain Philistine woman. On his way to visit her, a lion rushed out upon him from a neighboring thicket, and would have eaten him up, had not the spirit of God come upon him at the moment of greatest need, and enabled him, although unarmed, to seize and tear the lion to pieces.

SAMSON AND THE LION

Some time after, when passing along the same road, Samson saw a swarm of bees building their honeycombs in the lion's sun-dried carcass; and he ate some of the honey. As it was customary to ask riddles at marriage festivals, he gave the following to the Philistines when his own wedding took place:

"Out of the eater came forth meat, and out of the strong came forth sweetness."

The Philistines made vain efforts to find the answer of this riddle, and thus secure the prize of garments which Samson had promised them. At last, however, they coaxed the young man's bride to reveal the answer, and, going to him, triumphantly cried:

"What is sweeter than honey, and what is stronger than a lion?"

Samson, of course, was surprised to hear that they had solved his riddle; but when he found out that they had done so only by fraud, he was very indignant, and resolved to take his revenge. To pay the promised reward, therefore, he slew thirty Philistines, and gave their spoil to the wedding guests.

A few months later, when Samson would fain have claimed his wife, and taken her home, he was told that she had been given in marriage to another. To avenge this insult he tied firebrands to the tails of three hundred captive foxes, and then let the animals loose in the ripe grain fields. The grain soon caught fire, and all the Philistine harvest was destroyed.

In anger, the Philistines now burned Samson's wife and her father, and thereby so enraged the young man that he fell upon them, and "smote them hip and thigh with a great slaughter." Then he went and took refuge on the top of the rock of Etam in the territory of Judah.

CHAPTER XXXI

THE FALSE DELILAH

WE left Samson on top of a steep rock, where he had taken refuge after killing many Philistines to avenge his wife's death. Here he staid until he was captured by an army three thousand strong.

To prevent the escape of this prisoner, the men bound him securely with new ropes; but Samson broke them almost without effort. Then, seizing the jawbone of an ass lying near at hand, he wielded it so vigorously, and to such good purpose, that he soon stretched one thousand Philistines dead at his feet, and put to flight the remainder.

These superhuman efforts left Samson very weary, and he was so thirsty that he longed for a drink. To satisfy this want, a spring of fresh water suddenly and miraculously sprang out of the jawbone, and the thirsty hero was able to refresh himself.

This massacre of the Philistines was a cause of great rejoicing among the Israelites, who raised Samson to the rank of judge. In spite of this dignity, however, Samson continued to live as before, and he once ventured into

Gaza, one of the enemy's strongholds, to pay a visit there.

The Philistines, hearing that their foe was within their walls, closed the city gates, intending to find and kill Samson in the morning. But the hero, starting on his homeward journey at midnight, and finding the gates closed, lifted them off their hinges, and bore them off to the top of a neighboring mountain, whence the people of Gaza had much trouble in bringing them down once more.

Shortly after this adventure, Samson married another Philistine woman named Delilah. She had been secretly bribed by his enemies to discover the source of his great strength, and to deliver him into their hands securely fastened with bonds which even he could not break.

When first asked by his bride what bonds would hold him, Samson told her that he could not break green withes. So she once bound him thus, while he was asleep, and then awakened him by crying that the Philistines were coming; but he snapped his bonds as if they had been threads.

Delilah now made two other efforts to bind him,— once with new ropes, and once with seven strands of his own hair,—but these also failed to hold him. Then she pouted and coaxed until the giant told her that the real secret of his strength lay entirely in the keeping of his vow, and hence in his unshorn locks.

Delilah therefore cut off Samson's abundant hair while he was sound asleep, bound him, and delivered

DELILAH

him bodily into the hands of the cruel Philistines. They put out his eyes, and made him grind wheat in their prison.

Samson suffered untold agonies while thus in the enemy's power. But God had not entirely forsaken him; for, as his hair grew long again, he gradually felt his wonted strength come back.

His enemies, wishing to taunt him, once had him brought into the temple of their god Dagon. The heavy roof of this building was supported by large stone pillars. As it was a great festival, several thousand Philistines were assembled there on that occasion, and about three thousand were on the flat roof.

After breathing a short, silent prayer for divine help, Samson threw his powerful arms around two of the columns, gave them a mighty wrench, and thus tore them down. As they fell, the heavy roof which they supported came crashing down upon the heads of the luckless Philistines, whose taunts were still ringing in their victim's ears.

All the people assembled there perished, and Samson's body, taken from the ruins, was buried with his family in their ancestral burying ground.

CHAPTER XXXII

THE ARK CAPTURED

SAMSON was succeeded by Samuel, the last judge of Israel, and the first prophet of a long series which was continuous until the return from captivity in Babylon, as you will see.

Samuel was the son of a Levite and his wife, Hannah. This woman, having remained childless for many years, once went up to Shiloh to worship the Lord. She prayed so fervently before the altar that Eli, the high priest, concluded from her excited gestures that she must be the worse for strong drink.

He was about to turn her out of the holy place when she told him the cause of her grief. Eli then blessed her, and promised her a son. When Samuel was born, Hannah rejoiced greatly, but remembering the vow she had made to give her child to the Lord, she brought him to the temple as soon as he was weaned.

There the mother left her only son in the care of Eli, the high priest, and went home, where God rewarded her for her sacrifice by giving her three other sons and two daughters to cheer her old age.

Eli, the high priest, was a very good man, but very weak. Instead of training his sons, Hophni and Phinehas, in the way they should go, he treated them with such indulgence that they soon took to evil ways.

When the father saw this, he called his sons to him, reproached them for their bad conduct, and sadly compared them to Samuel, who "was in favor both with the Lord and also with men." But this reproof came too late, and the young men went on doing wrong, until a prophet came to tell Eli that both his sons would die on the same day, and that instead of them God would find a priest worthy of serving him.

Eli was already very old and nearly blind. He dwelt in the temple, where he once laid himself down to sleep in his chamber. Near him, but in another room, lay Samuel, and there the voice of the Lord suddenly called the child.

With cheerful readiness, Samuel answered, "Here am I." He thought that the aged high priest had called him, so he ran into Eli's room to ask his wishes. "But Eli sent Samuel back to bed, thinking that he had been dreaming. The call was twice repeated, and at last the priest bade Samuel answer, should he hear the voice again, "Speak, Lord, for thy servant heareth." Once more the voice fell upon Samuel's listening ear, and when he had answered, according to Eli's orders, the Lord said that he would execute judgment upon the sons of Eli, who would die in punishment for their sins.

When morning came, Eli called Samuel to him, and asked what the Lord had said. Samuel now reluctantly repeated the words he had heard, and the old man, whose heart was broken with grief, bowed his head and cried: "It is the Lord; let him do what seemeth him good."

From that day Samuel was a prophet of the Lord, and he silently watched the Israelites, who were gathering their forces together; for they had decided to make a great effort to free themselves from the hated yoke of the Philistines.

In the very first battle, however, the Israelites were defeated, and lost four thousand men. Eli's sons, Hophni and Phinehas, thought that they might be more successful if they only had the Ark in their midst; so they now brought it into camp, although they had no authority for doing so.

The Israelites, who remembered the miracle of the Jordan and the falling of the walls of Jericho, received the Ark with loud shouts of joy. But this gladness was soon turned into mourning; for, in the very next battle, the Philistines, fighting with the energy of despair, killed Hophni and Phinehas, together with thousands of their followers, and gained possession of the precious Ark.

They bore this treasure off in triumph,—for they knew the immense importance it had in the eyes of the Israelites,—and placed it as a trophy in the temple of Dagon, their principal god, who was half man and half fish.

The news of the Israelites' defeat and great loss was quickly carried to Shiloh by a soldier who managed to escape from the general massacre. He presented himself before Eli, with torn garments and with earth on his head, in token of great mourning.

The high priest was silent and apparently unmoved, as he heard of the death of his sons and the destruction of the army; but when the messenger added that the Ark of God had fallen into the enemy's hands, Eli fell back from his seat and died.

That same day, the young wife of Phinehas heard the mournful tidings, and gave birth to a son, whom she called Ichabod ("where is the glory?"), because with the loss of the sacred Ark she said, "The glory is departed from Israel."

CHAPTER XXXIII

THE RETURN OF THE ARK

THE Philistines, who had won such a brilliant victory, and had secured such a fine prize, were beside themselves with joy. But when they again entered their temple, this joy was changed into amazement; for they found their god lying in fragments at the foot of the Ark.

Soon after, all the men of the city became ill, and hosts of mice overran the land, causing great damage. They soon blamed the Ark for these misfortunes, and carried it elsewhere; but wherever it went, plagues and calamities went with it. Weary of suffering, the Philistines finally made up their minds to send the Ark back to the Israelites.

Under the direction of their priests, they made golden emblems of their plagues, placed them in a coffer of precious wood, and set it with the Ark upon a new cart, to which they harnessed two young cows that had never yet borne the yoke.

These animals were allowed to go as they pleased, and soon turned into the road leading to Beth-shemesh, slowly followed by five Philistine lords, who wished to see what would happen. The cart passed near some harvest fields, where the Israelites were working, and when they saw the Ark they rejoiced aloud.

Then the Levites came forward and took possession of the treasure. They used the cart for firewood and the cows for victims, and offered up a sacrifice of thanksgiving for the miraculous return of the Ark which they had lost.

But some of the men, having ventured to peer into the Ark in idle curiosity, were slain. When the people of Beth-shemesh saw this, they were afraid to keep the Ark among them, and begged the men of Kirjathjearim to take it into their city. This request was cheerfully complied with, and the Ark remained there for many years, causing many blessings to fall upon the house under whose roof it had found shelter.

The Israelites had failed to shake off the Philistine yoke as easily as they expected; so they now gladly listened to Samuel's advice, and began to repent of their sins. To recover the favor of God, they set aside the idols which they worshiped. Then they came together at Mizpeh and implored Samuel to pray aloud in their behalf.

In the very midst of this prayer, their old enemies, the Philistines, fell upon them. But this time the Lord was with his people, and he sent a sudden and timely thunderstorm, which filled the hearts of the Philistines with superstitious dread. They were so terrified that they turned and fled, and thus the Israelites won an easy victory.

This battle put an end to the Philistine oppression, which had lasted forty years; and Samuel, growing old, now judged Israel with the help of his two sons. The prophet dwelt at Ramah, where the people often came to consult him, because they knew that he could give them very good advice.

The end of Samuel's long life was clouded on account of the bad behavior of his sons, and because of the persistent request of the elders that he would give them a king. They said that they wanted such a ruler to defend them in case of new attacks on the part of their enemies.

Samuel vainly tried to convince the elders that God was the best king, and that the theocracy under which they lived was the very best system of government for them; they would not believe him. So Samuel, warned by God that it would be well to give the people their own way, finally told them that he would soon choose a king for them.

A few days later, a young man named Saul came to the prophet to ask where he could find his father's asses, which had wandered out of their pasture and were lost. Advised by God, Samuel led the man into his own house, told him that the asses were already found, and, after detaining him over night, started out with him on his homeward journey on the morrow.

CHAPTER XXXIV

SAUL, KING OF ISRAEL

SAMUEL and Saul had not gone very far before the prophet bade the young man send his servant on ahead. When the man had gone, and they were alone, Samuel told Saul to stop, and took out "a vial of oil, and poured it upon his head, and kissed him." This was to show that he took Saul for his king.

As Saul seemed to be somewhat amazed and doubtful, Samuel told him that he had been made king by God's will, and that as a proof he would soon hear of the safety of his father's asses, would receive a present, and would be inspired by the spirit of the Lord to utter a prophecy.

All these things happened just as Samuel had foretold; and the people, hearing Saul prophesy for the first time, exclaimed in wonder: "Is Saul also among the prophets?" The new king did not immediately assume his royal state, however, but returned quietly to his father's house.

Not very long after this event, Samuel called all the elders of the people together, and bade them select their king by lot. Their choice also fell upon Saul; but when his name was called, he was nowhere to be seen, although he was taller than any one else. It seems that he had hidden himself through modesty; but the people at once began to search for him, and he was soon forced to come out from his hiding place.

Saul was led into the very midst of the assembled people and was welcomed with the cheer: "God save the king!" So far as we know, this is the first time that writers mention this cry, which has since been heard many times and in many countries.

Escorted by a volunteer bodyguard, Saul went home to Gibeah, where he quietly staid until the people of another town begged him to save them from the hands of their enemies, the Ammonites, who kept them closely besieged.

Prompted by the spirit of God, Saul now collected an army of three hundred and thirty thousand men, fell suddenly upon the Ammonites, and completely defeated them. Then he went to Gilgal, where Samuel publicly laid down his charge as judge, and gave the people over to Saul's care.

Although the great army had gone home, Saul soon raised a new force of three thousand men, with which he proceeded to make war on the enemies of Israel. In this work he was greatly helped by his son Jonathan, a young man of great valor.

Saul's small army was once encamped at Gilgal, when they became frightened at the numbers of the enemy, and postponed an attack, intending to wait until Samuel could come and offer up a prayer in their behalf.

But Samuel did not come as soon as he was expected; so Saul became impatient, and decided that he would offer up the sacrifice, although he knew that he had no right to do so.

Saul had just finished this religious ceremony when Samuel appeared. The prophet, who knew that the king had done wrong, now reproved him, and foretold that in punishment for this sin the crown would not long remain in his hands, and would never belong to his children.

When Saul heard these words, he was troubled and ashamed, and did not dare to begin the war. The Philistines, seeing this, spread rapidly over the country, and took away all the weapons that the Israelites had. Then they carried away all the smiths, and thus forced the Chosen People to come into their enemy's camp to have even their tools sharpened.

This tyranny soon became so unbearable that Jonathan resolved to end it. Accompanied only by his armor-bearer, he boldly entered the Philistine camp, and slew many men. A timely earthquake, occurring at the same moment, bewildered the Philistines so sorely that they fell upon one another with drawn swords. Their own work of destruction was then finished by the Israelites, who crept out of the caves where they had taken refuge, and joined in the slaughter with hearty good will.

This massacre was finally seen from Saul's camp, and he gave his men orders to follow the fugitives, rashly adding: "Cursed be the man that eateth any food until evening." Saul said these words, intending to show his men that they must pursue the enemy without stopping for rest or refreshment; and he little thought that the curse would fall upon his own son.

It seems that Jonathan had not heard his father's command; and, in passing through a forest, he dipped his rod in a honeycomb, and put it to his mouth. This act of disobedience was soon discovered by Saul, who would have punished it by death, as he had vowed, had not all the people insisted that their favorite Jonathan must live.

CHAPTER XXXV

THE ANOINTING OF DAVID

THE campaign against the Philistines was followed by a long series of victories over the Moabites, Ammonites, Edomites, and Amalekites, and Saul, having subdued all his enemies, could at last assume the royal state. But even in the midst of his splendor he could not forget Samuel's prophecy, and kept wondering how he could secure the crown to his descendants.

From time to time the prophet Samuel still appeared at the king's court, to bring him God's commands, and on one occasion he bade Saul fight the Amalekites, and utterly destroy them and all their possessions. Instead of obeying this order faithfully, Saul carried it out only in part; for he divided the best of the spoil among his people, and spared the life of Agag, the King of the Amalekites.

But on the way home Saul was met by Samuel, to whom God had said: "It repenteth me that I have set up Saul to be king." When Samuel reproved Saul for his disobedience, the king vainly tried to excuse himself by saying that he had saved the cattle to offer up in sacrifice; but the prophet would not listen to him.

Then Samuel went on to tell Saul that on account of his disobedience, he would no longer be helped by God. Terrified by these words, the king now clung to the prophet's mantle, imploring forgiveness for his sins, until a piece of the garment was torn off and remained in his hands.

The prophet made use of this accident to illustrate the meaning of his words, and said: "The Lord hath rent the kingdom of Israel from thee this day, and hath given it to a neighbor of thine that is better than thou." But before leaving court, Samuel himself saw that God's commands were fully obeyed, by sending for the captive king Agag, and cutting off his head.

This was Samuel's last visit to Saul, whom the Lord had now forsaken; but the prophet mourned this king's disobedience so sorely that God reproved him. At the same time the Lord bade Samuel take a vial of oil, and go to the house of Jesse, the grandson of Ruth, where he would find the new king.

Samuel obeyed, and when he had reached Jesse's house, he asked to see the man's sons. Seven of Ruth's stalwart great-grandsons passed before the prophet, but it was only when David, the eighth and youngest, appeared, that the divine voice spoke to Samuel, saying: "Arise, anoint him, for this is he."

No sooner had this future king been anointed, in the midst of his family, than the spirit of the Lord forsook Saul and fell upon David. From that moment, too, Saul seemed possessed at times by an evil spirit which drove him to wild acts.

DAVID

The anointing of David was Samuel's last public deed before he finally withdrew to his home at Ramah. But David resumed his peaceful occupation as shepherd, and learned to sing and play, a talent which later won for him the title of "Sweet Singer in Israel." Then, too, he gave the first signs of the dauntless courage, which was to distinguish him all through life, and bravely defended his flocks from the attacks of lions and bears, and even of Philistine thieves.

All through the reign of Saul, the Israelites were forced to contend with the Philistines. These enemies of the Chosen People grew bolder and bolder, and when the spirit of the Lord forsook the king, they began to get the better of him. Encouraged by success, they finally assembled all their forces at a mountain in the Israelite territory, where Saul came with his army to oppose them.

In the ranks of the Israelites there were three of Jesse's sons, and David frequently came down to visit them. It was in the course of one of these brief sojourns with the army, that he once saw a Philistine giant step forth, and heard him boastfully challenge the Israelites to single combat.

No one accepted the challenge, until, moved by the spirit of the Lord, David offered to fight the giant. As soon as this offer was made known, David was led into the presence of Saul, where he firmly declared that God, who had "delivered him out of the paw of the lion and out of the paw of the bear," would surely save him from the hand of the giant Philistine.

CHAPTER XXXVI

DAVID AND GOLIATH

WHEN Saul heard David firmly, yet modestly, assert his trust in the help of the Lord, he no longer dared oppose the youth; so he not only allowed David to go forth and fight, but even offered to lend him some costly armor, and helped him to put on the cuirass and helmet.

The young shepherd, however, was not used to the weight of arms, and he staggered and nearly fell when in full battle array. Seeing that such an outfit was not for him, David now said that he would rather meet the giant with nothing but his shepherd's staff and the sling which he handled with great skill.

After choosing a few smooth stones down by a brook, the boyish champion went boldly forth to meet the Philistine warrior, whose name was Goliath. This giant viewed David's approach with great scorn, and began to taunt him, but all his boasts were soon silenced by a swift stone from David's sling, which pierced his forehead and sank into his brain.

When Goliath fell, David sprang forward, and, seizing the giant's huge sword, used it to cut off his head.

The Philistines, seeing that their champion warrior had fallen, turned and fled in sudden dismay; but they were soon pursued and slaughtered without mercy by the Israelite army.

David's courage and skill roused the admiration of all the nation, and even of Saul's daughter, whose hand was promised him in marriage in reward for his bravery. The marriage was not to take place at once, however, and in the mean while David was called upon to soothe the king's outbursts of wrath by the sweet tones of his voice and harp.

At first Saul listened to his harper with delight, but little by little he grew jealous of the bright youth whom everybody praised. Soon he overheard the people exalting the young warrior, and saying: "Saul hath slain his thousands, and David his ten thousands," and then his wicked envy gained the upper hand.

In a fit of rage the mad king therefore once flung his spear at the youth, while he was playing his harp, but fortunately the weapon missed the mark. A second similar attempt was equally fruitless; and Saul, seeing that he could not kill David, now resolved to insult him.

Instead of giving David his daughter's hand in marriage, as he had promised, Saul bestowed her upon another suitor. Then, finding that Michal, his younger daughter, had fallen in love with David, he told the youth that he might have her if he would kill one hundred Philistines. This condition was made because Saul hoped that David would fall by the hand of the enemy; but the young man went forth, slew two hundred Philistines, and, securing their spoil, came and laid it at Saul's feet, claiming his promised bride.

As no further pretext could be found to delay the marriage, Saul gave his daughter Michal to David, as he had promised.

But although he had thus been forced to acknowledge David's services, Saul still hated his son-in-law, and he once bade his courtiers and his son Jonathan kill the young hero.

Jonathan was faithful to David, his chosen friend, and therefore interceded for him, and succeeded in partly disarming Saul's wrath. But when a new fit of madness came upon the king, his anger all returned, and he hired assassins to steal into David's room and murder him in his sleep.

Warned by Michal of the threatening danger, David fled secretly and by night, while his wife deceived the murderers by making the image of a man and placing it in her husband's bed.

CHAPTER XXXVII

DAVID'S FLIGHT

DAVID had narrowly escaped death on several occasions, as we have seen, and now he did not dare return to the king's palace. He therefore withdrew to a place near Ramah, where Saul's messengers soon came to take him prisoner. They did not dare do so, however; for on the way the spirit of the Lord came upon them, and forced them to prophesy against their will.

When Saul heard of the utter failure of this attempt to secure David, he himself went out in search of him; but being overcome on the way by the spirit of the Lord, he too dared do no harm, and merely invited his son-in-law to return to court.

David did not know whether he could trust to Saul's apparent friendship, so he had a secret interview with Jonathan. The king's son gladly offered to find out whether it would be safe for David to return, and to give him timely warning should any immediate danger threaten him.

Jonathan, feeling sure from his father's actions that David was still viewed with dislike, soon went out into a field where he knew that David was hiding. As he did not dare seek his friend openly, he made believe to practice shooting; for he had agreed with David that his orders to the lad who picked up his arrows would be intended as information whether or not the king could be trusted.

David, therefore, listened attentively, and learned that he must fly; but after the lad had gone, Jonathan drew near the hiding place, to take a brief but affectionate farewell of his dearest friend.

In obedience to the advice which he had thus obtained from Jonathan, David quickly fled. As he was unarmed and without provisions, he made use of a stratagem to secure food and a sword. He entered the house of the high priest, and pretended that he was the bearer of a message from Saul, and that his servants were waiting for him near by. Then he asked for and obtained the sword of Goliath, and five of the sacred loaves of shew-bread, which the priests alone were allowed to eat.

Thus armed and refreshed, David made his way to the court of a certain Philistine king, where a new danger threatened him, and where he escaped death only by pretending to be crazy.

From this place David soon passed on to the cave of Adullam, where he dwelt for some time. He was joined here by his brothers, and by a large force of Israelites, who, displeased with the actions of their king, now took sides against him.

To prevent Saul's harming his parents in any way,

David secretly led them into the land of Moab, where he left them under the protection of the king. Then, fearing nothing for himself, he set out with four hundred men to wage war on his own account with his old enemies, the Philistines.

While he was thus an outcast and a wanderer, David met with many adventures, only a few of which are recorded in the Bible. For instance, three of his followers once cut their way through the Philistine camp, which surrounded them on all sides, merely to get some water to quench his thirst.

But David was too generous a man to enjoy a drink secured at the risk of his friends' lives; and, to prevent their ever venturing forth thus rashly again, he poured it all out on the ground, exclaiming reproachfully: "Shall I drink the blood of these men that have put their lives in jeopardy?"

While he was living in the cave of Adullam, David once received a visit from the prophet Gad, who bade him go into the land of Judah. But no sooner had David done so, than Saul came after him to make another attempt to kill him.

On the way, Saul heard for the first time that the high priest had seen David, and had helped him in his flight. In his anger at this news, Saul had the priest and eighty-five of his assistants slain, as well as all the citizens of the unfortunate town where they lived.

Only one of them, Abiathar, son of the high priest, managed to escape from the general massacre. Fleeing for his life, he joined David, who now bitterly repented of his deception, and mourned over the terrible consequences which had resulted from it.

Advised by Abiathar and Gad, the high priest and the prophet, David began to fight against the Philistines. He defeated them with great slaughter, and then remained at the city of Keilah until warned by God that the men of that place were about to betray him into Saul's hands.

CHAPTER XXXVIII

DAVID'S GENEROSITY

FORCED to leave Keilah because he could no longer trust the people around him, David now fled into the wilderness, where Saul vainly sought him. Here David had a last interview with Jonathan, who assured him that he would in time be king over all Israel.

Then, still pursued by Saul, David fled on; and he would surely have been made prisoner, had not the king been turned aside by a sudden raid on the part of the Philistines. While Saul was waging war against these old foes, David made his way to Engedi.

But as soon as the war with the Philistines was ended, Saul resumed the pursuit of David, and, coming to Engedi, he stopped to rest in a cave. He slept there peacefully, little suspecting that the foe whom he had come to seek lay but a few feet from him.

While the king slept in the midst of his guard, David noiselessly stole out of the dark recesses of the cave where he had been hiding. He stole up to the sleeping king, and cut off a piece of the royal mantle, which he bore off as a trophy when he went away.

When Saul and his army were riding off on the morrow, David suddenly appeared at the mouth of the cave and showed him the piece of his garment. The young man urged that this was a good proof of his innocence, seeing that he had not tried to harm the king when it was in his power to do so.

Saul, touched by the generosity of David, who could so easily have killed him in his sleep, now gave up all thought of harming his son-in-law, and cried: "Thou art more righteous than I; for thou hast rewarded me good, whereas I have rewarded thee evil."

As the pursuit was thus ended for the time being, David supported himself for a while by the gifts of neighboring farmers, whom, in exchange, he protected from the raids of their enemies. On one occasion David sent ten young men to the farm of Nabal, to ask for the usual provisions. But Nabal churlishly refused to give any, and would have been punished sorely by David and his angry troops, had not his wife, Abigail, hastened to appease their wrath.

She took an ample supply of food, and brought it to David in person; then, falling at his feet, she implored him to spare her husband and family. Pleased by her gifts, and touched by her beauty, David consented; and when Nabal died, he took Abigail for his wife, for Michal, the king's daughter, had during his absence been given in marriage to another man.

The memory of David's generosity did not linger long in Saul's mind, so we soon hear of his starting out again to seize and kill David. But the young hero,

DAVID AND SAUL

accompanied by only one servant, slipped one night into the king's camp and tent, and left it unseen, carrying off Saul's spear and cup.

When he reached a hill opposite the sleeping army, David raised his voice and awoke the sleepers. Then, holding up his trophies in full sight of them all, he again told Saul what he had done. As in the meeting at the cave of Engedi, Saul felt touched by David's kindness in sparing his life, and, instead of continuing the pursuit, went away, after he had sent one of his soldiers to get his spear and cup, as David bade him.

David and Saul never saw each other again, after this strange conversation from one hilltop to another; for, fearing that the king would again forget his solemn promise, David went away with all his followers to take refuge among his old enemies, the Philistines. They were so glad to get the help of so good a warrior that they gave him a city to live in. David dwelt here for about one year, fighting with great success against the Amalekites and other tribes, and bringing back much spoil.

The King of the Philistines was so pleased with his share of the booty that he treated David as a friend, and told him all his secrets. One day he even made known to him a plan which he had made to attack the Israelites, and asked him to join the army. David did not dare to refuse, but when the other Philistines heard what the king had done, they would not let David fight with them, and had him sent back to his town.

CHAPTER XXXIX

DAVID MADE KING

SAUL, in the mean while, had heard that the Philistines were coming, and he was very anxious to know how the war would end. As the spirit of the Lord had left him, and he could not find out what would happen in any other way, he now made up his mind to do as many people did then, and consult a witch.

Saul had often rebuked the Israelites for doing this, and as they did not heed him he had killed nearly all the witches in his land some time before. Only one had escaped him, and she now dwelt at Endor, where Saul went in disguise to ask her advice.

The witch soon recognized the king, although he came without his usual train of followers; but, after making him promise that he would not harm her in any way, she consented to use her magic arts in his presence. By spells and incantations she then called up the spirit of the prophet Samuel, whom Saul said he wished to see.

Saul questioned the spirit when it rose up before him, and learned not only that his army would meet with a terrible defeat, but that he and his sons would perish on that same fatal day.

In a gloomy frame of mind he left the witch of Endor, and went forth to meet the Philistines. As Samuel's wraith had foretold, the Israelites were beaten, and Saul's sons were killed. Then the king and his armor-bearer, unwilling to survive and become the prisoners of their foes, fell upon their swords and died also.

David, coming back to his town among the Philistines after a short absence, now found that the Amalekites had taken and burned it, and had carried off his two wives, Abigail and Ahinoam. After consulting the high priest Abiathar, and getting his leave to fight, David pursued and defeated the Amalekites, and gave their spoil to his own followers. As he came back to his own town, he was met by a messenger, an eyewitness of the terrible battle between the Philistines and the Israelites.

This man told David about the defeat of the Israelites and the death of the king and his sons. Then, hoping to win David's favor, he added that it was he that had killed Saul with his own hand. This untruth received a speedy punishment; for David, believing it, bade one of his soldiers cut off the man's head.

The death of all the royal family was a great blow to David, but he mourned especially for his friend Jonathan. Several of his psalms, which bear the impress of his grief, are supposed to have been composed at this time, and to be a sort of funeral lament for the royal race.

The whole country was in a terrible condition at this time. Although Abner, general-in-chief of the Israelite army, had proclaimed Ishbosheth, the youngest son of Saul, as king, the Philistines had taken possession of the greater part of the country.

For two years Ishbosheth made a feeble attempt to reign; but Abner saw that David's party daily became more powerful, so he finally proposed to make peace with him and join him. David accepted these proposals, and promised to receive Abner kindly, provided that his wife Michal was given back to him.

All would have gone well, and the two parties would have been good friends, had not Joab, David's captain, slain Abner soon after he left his master's presence. This act of treachery so angered David that he cursed Joab and all his family, and mourned publicly for the murdered Abner.

When the rest of the people saw how just David was, they all said that they were in favor of him. Two captains then slew Ishbosheth and carried his head to David, from whom they expected a reward. But David, who despised all treachery, put them both to death.

Although some members of Saul's family were left, David was now called sole king; and he reigned at Hebron seven and a half years before he moved to Jerusalem. In this new capital, "David went on, and grew great, for the Lord God of hosts was with him." It was here, too, that Hiram, King of Tyre, sent to ask his alliance, promising him in exchange cedar wood from Mount Lebanon for the building of a new palace at Jerusalem.

This palace was very grand and spacious; for David, not content with Michal, Abigail, and Ahinoam, had many other wives, and was the father of many children, who all dwelt under his own roof.

CHAPTER XL

THE ARK BROUGHT TO JERUSALEM

DAVID was soon obliged to leave his new capital, to go forth and fight his old foes, the Philistines. When he had conquered these enemies, he felt that it was time to bring the Ark of the Covenant to Jerusalem, and to build a temple where it might take up its abode for good. With an escort of thirty thousand men, he therefore set out. The Ark was placed on a new cart, driven by the sons of the high priest, and the procession slowly wended its way towards Jerusalem.

God had commanded that no one should venture to touch the Ark while on its way, but one of the high priest's sons stretched out his hand to steady it when the cart tipped. No sooner had he touched it than he fell down dead.

Awed by this accident, the king ordered the journey stopped, and the Ark was placed for safe keeping in a house near by, where it remained three months. Then, seeing that it brought great blessings to the place where it was kept, the people again became anxious to have it in Jerusalem; and as soon as the new tent, or tabernacle, was finished, they sent the Levites to bring it thither.

To show his respect for the God of Israel, David went ahead of the Ark on foot, in the simple garb of a minstrel; and, dancing and playing upon his harp, he led the way to Mount Zion, where the Ark was to remain.

In his joy at the recovery of this precious Ark, David also gave alms to all the poor, and he offered up costly sacrifices. His joy was marred, however, when Michal, his wife, taunted him for dancing and singing before his people. David finally grew so angry with her that he sent her away from him forever.

Although David had thus safely brought the sacred Ark to Jerusalem, and had placed it in the new tabernacle, he did not consider a tent a sufficiently handsome abode, and wished to build a fine temple for it.

But when he consulted the prophet Nathan, he learned that the honor of building this temple was reserved for one of his sons. He also received a renewal of the old promise of the birth of the Messiah. This promise gave him great pleasure, and was the probable source of the joyful psalms which are known as the Messianic psalms.

As David did not dare to undertake the building of the temple after Nathan's words, he made use of his time in completing the defeat of the Philistines. Then, too, he punished the Moabites for the treacherous murder of his parents, whom he had left in their care.

David also made war against the Edomites, one of whose young princes fled to Egypt. There he grew up and plotted revenge, coming back to Palestine with a mighty army in the days of the next king, Solomon.

By all these victories, which are celebrated in some of the psalms, David little by little enlarged his kingdom, till it reached as far as the banks of the Red Sea. All the Promised Land now belonged to the Chosen People; but their hold on it was rather uncertain, because they had not always been faithful to the Lord.

David was now so firmly placed upon the throne that he no longer feared the family of Saul. He even received Saul's last descendants in his palace, where he made them welcome and treated them like his own sons.

But the consequences of Saul's sins were not yet ended. Because he had murdered the Gibeonites, a great famine came over the land a few years later, and lasted three years, causing much suffering. David, hoping to end this famine, finally offered to give the Gibeonites satisfaction, and in answer to their demands he gave up into their hands seven of the former king's family. The Gibeonites, like most people of the time, believed in revenge; so they hung these seven men on the hill of Gibeon, and decreed that their corpses should swing there for several months.

Rizpah, the distracted mother of two of the dead, wished to protect their bodies from the beaks and claws of the vultures and other birds of prey, so she took up her position at the foot of the gallows. There she wildly

RIZPAH PROTECTING THE BODIES OF HER SONS

strove to drive away the birds by day and the wild beasts by night, until David, touched by her devotion, had the bodies taken down and buried.

CHAPTER XLI

THE REPENTANCE OF DAVID

ALTHOUGH the wars with the enemies of Israel were not yet entirely ended, David left the army to the care of Joab, and came back to his capital, Jerusalem. It was while looking out of his palace window one day, that he saw a beautiful woman at her toilet, and fell deeply in love with her.

He now asked who she was, and soon found out that her name was Bathsheba, and that she was the wife of Uriah, one of his soldiers. As David wanted to have this beautiful woman for his own wife, he began to plot how he could get rid of her husband, Uriah; for he knew very well that he could marry her only after she was a widow.

After much thought, David decided on a plan. He sent word to the captain of his army to place Uriah in such an exposed spot, when the next battle took place, that he would surely be killed. The captain obeyed, Uriah fell, and David soon married Bathsheba, the widow, whom he had thus won by the greatest crime of his life.

Of course so wicked a deed as this greatly displeased

the Lord, and he sent Nathan, one of his prophets, to reprove the king. Nathan came before David, and, to make sure that he would listen, began to tell this parable:

There was once upon a time a poor man, who had only one ewe lamb. He fed this little creature out of his hand, and cared for it very tenderly both night and day. Near this poor man there dwelt a rich farmer, who had great flocks, and more lambs than he could count.

One day a stranger came to visit the rich man, and the latter gave orders that a feast should be made ready for his guest. As there was no meat in the house, he bade his servant go catch the poor man's pet lamb and kill it, so that they might have enough to eat.

David listened attentively to this story, and was very angry when he heard that the rich man, instead of killing one of his own lambs, had taken the poor man's pet. He said that such a thing was mean, unjust, and cruel, and vowed that the rich man should be severely punished.

But when he sternly asked Nathan: "Who is the man?" he was astonished and ashamed to hear the answer: "Thou art the man." The prophet then went on to explain that, while the king's heart had been filled with pity for the poor man who had lost a pet lamb, he had felt no such feelings for Uriah, whom he had killed, and whose wife he had married.

David now understood how deeply he had sinned, and he repented greatly. He prayed to God to forgive him, and, as he was a poet, he composed a number of psalms, or hymns, which he used to sing, accompanying himself on his harp. In these poems he expressed his sorrow and deep repentance; hence they are called the "penitential psalms."

But in spite of his repentance David could not escape all punishment, and the first child which Bathsheba bore him fell very sick. The king loved this child dearly; so he fasted and prayed, and was so anxious that when it breathed its last the courtiers did not at first dare tell him that it was dead.

But when David heard that the child had ceased to live and suffer, he became very calm, and left off weeping and fasting. His courtiers, who had expected a great outburst of grief, were amazed at his calmness. Finally they ventured to ask him how he could be so composed, now that the child was dead, when the mere knowledge of its danger had made him spend all his time in fasting and prayer.

David then sadly told them that as long as the little one lived, he had hoped by prayers and tears to make God forgive his sin, and leave him the child. But when he heard that it was dead, he knew that tears were useless, and added softly: "I shall go to him, but he shall not return to me."

CHAPTER XLII

ABSALOM IN DISGRACE

BATHSHEBA and David were slightly comforted for the loss of their first child by the birth of another son, whom they called Solomon, which means "peace." They gave him this name because the wars were just ended, and a peace had begun which David hoped would last a very long while.

He was mistaken, however. The peace did not last; for God wished to punish David for his sins, and especially for having caused the death of Uriah; so he stirred up great troubles for the king. Even David's many children now quarreled together, and one of them, Amnon, insulted Tamar, his half-sister.

This young prince was not bad by nature, but, unfortunately, he liked to associate with bad companions. They soon taught him to be as wicked and mean as themselves, and after he had wronged his stepsister, they encouraged him to turn her out of the house and into the street.

Tamar was weeping bitterly when her brother Absalom found her, and when he heard how shamefully she had been treated, he took her into his own house, and vowed that he would avenge her.

Although Absalom was now always seeking for a chance to punish Amnon, he had to wait a very long while before he could do so. At the end of two years, however, he made a great feast, to which he invited all the king's sons.

Amnon came with the other guests, and sat with them at meat, little thinking that his end was so near. But in the middle of the feast, Absalom's servants suddenly fell upon him and killed him, before he could make an attempt to defend himself. The other princes, seeing Amnon fall, rushed out of the room, and, mounting their mules, rode quickly away, lest the same fate should overtake them.

Absalom had at last avenged his sister Tamar, but, fearing David's displeasure, he did not dare return to court; so he went to live elsewhere during the next three years. The king, who had always treated Absalom as a favorite, secretly longed to see him, but did not like to recall him, because he had done wrong and because there was danger that the people might injure him. Joab, the general of the army, felt sure that David was very anxious to forgive his son, yet hardly knew how to do so, and at last he sent an old woman to see the king and tell him this story:

"I am a poor woman, a widow, and I had two sons. They were a great comfort to me; but, unfortunately, while working out in the fields one day, they began to quarrel and soon came to blows. As no one was there to stop them, they fought until one was killed by accident.

"All my relatives are so angry at the only son I now have left, that they wish to kill him to avenge his brother; and thus they would leave me all alone in the world."

The king, touched by the poor woman's sorrow, bade her weep no more. He promised that her son should be allowed to come home, and that no one would dare to do him any harm.

Then the woman confessed to the king that the story she had told him was not true, and also that she had spoken by Joab's order. But she had made the king understand that, provided he were willing to forgive his son Absalom, no one would dare to oppose him.

David now saw that the wisest plan would be to send for Absalom, who, therefore, came back to Jerusalem to live. But although Absalom had thus been recalled by his father, David refused to see him, and the young man began to make many friends among the people who did not like the king.

One of these men, the king's own counselor, secretly advised Absalom to try to become king in his father's stead, and encouraged the prince to form a plot which resulted in forcing David to flee from Jerusalem in great haste.

David fled from his capital, followed by a small band of devoted men, and the Levites came after him with the Ark of God. But David soon bade the priests carry it back into the city, saying that, if the Lord wished, he would yet be brought back to Jerusalem, where he would again see the Ark.

As David passed along, weeping, he was soon overtaken by another faithful servant, Hushai. In obedience to the king's orders, this man went back to Jerusalem, and pretended to join Absalom, only in order to discover and defeat all the prince's plans.

A little further on, the king was met by Shimei, a member of Saul's house, who stoned and insulted him. David bore this harsh treatment with humility, and would not allow his servant to punish Shimei. He sadly said that it was the just punishment of his many sins.

While David was thus fleeing, Absalom triumphantly entered Jerusalem, where he graciously accepted the services of Hushai, and settled himself comfortably in his father's palace.

CHAPTER XLIII

THE DEATH OF ABSALOM

A S Absalom lingered in Jerusalem to enjoy the pleasures of royalty, David had time to assemble an army on the other side of the Jordan, and to place it under the command of Joab and two other generals.

The king then called all three of these men into his presence, and, after giving them his general orders, he added: "Deal gently for my sake with the young man, even with Absalom." Thus, you see, he still loved his rebellious son dearly, and was very anxious that Absalom should meet with no harm.

The armies started out, and met Absalom in a great forest, where his host was defeated. The prince, seeing that the battle was lost, then fled in haste through the forest, until the mule which he rode carried him under the spreading branches of an oak tree.

Absalom's long, fluttering hair caught in the branches of this tree, and he hung there while his mule dashed on. The pursuers, headed by Joab, soon found Absalom, and, forgetful of the king's charge, they killed him.

The news of the victory soon came to David, but

all his joy was changed to grief when he heard that Absalom, his favorite son, was dead. The aged king "went up to the chamber over the gate, and wept; and as he wept, thus he said: 'O my son Absalom, my son, my son Absalom! Would God I had died for thee, O Absalom, my son, my son!' "

The poor father continued mourning thus, until his captain Joab bade him rouse himself, and make an effort to win back his kingdom, unless he wished to lose the people's affection forever.

David, understanding the importance of this advice, then set aside his private sorrows, made a treaty with the rebels, and went back to Jerusalem in triumph. There Shimei was one of the first to come and ask his pardon for the stones and insults which he had hurled against him when he left Jerusalem in sorrow.

The joy of the king's return to his capital was soon marred by a quarrel between the tribes of Benjamin and Judah, and by the jealousy of Joab and Amasa. This Amasa had just been appointed captain of the army, so he started out to fight the Benjamites.

Joab, who was unwilling to give up the command of the troops, now secretly followed Amasa, and, after killing him, headed the army as usual, and pursued the Benjamites to a city far to the north. There, seeing that they would not otherwise be able to escape from Joab's wrath, the people killed the rebel leader, and flung his head over the wall and into the camp.

As we have seen, David had already been punished for his sins by a three years' famine, and an exile from

Jerusalem which lasted three months. He had sorely repented, but he soon fell into another sin as bad as the rest; for in spite of God's command, he counted the Israelites so that he might glory in their numbers.

The punishment came almost as soon as the census was ended; for a prophet of the Lord came to David, bidding him choose among three evils the one he would rather endure,—seven years of famine, three months of flight, or three days of pestilence. Having tested the first two punishments, and knowing full well what sufferings they had brought upon him and his people, David chose the last, as the least evil of the three. So the angel of destruction passed over the city, and in three days no less than seventy thousand people died of the plague.

By the advice of a prophet, David then built an altar upon the spot where the angel had stood, and there he offered up sacrifices, day and night, until the plague had ceased. It was upon this spot that the temple was built during the next reign, and from this time on David amassed a large treasure for that purpose.

Everybody knew that David wished Solomon to succeed him, but not all the people were satisfied with this choice. A conspiracy was therefore formed to set another son on the throne in Solomon's stead as soon as David died.

The news of this plot came to the ears of the prophet Nathan, and of Bathsheba, who therefore coaxed David to have Solomon anointed as his successor during his lifetime. This ceremony took place in public, and in it the priest used the sacred oil which was kept in the tabernacle for this purpose only.

Having reigned forty years, secured a fine capital, amassed wealth enough for the future temple, anointed his successor, and given him good advice, David now died "full of days, riches, and honor; and Solomon, his son, reigned in his stead."

CHAPTER XLIV

THE JUDGMENT OF SOLOMON

UNDER the reign of Solomon, the Jewish kingdom reached its highest point of glory and power. The new king had inherited from his father not only an extensive country, but also very great wealth. He was, besides, very clever, and had been well educated by his mother, Bathsheba, and by the prophet Nathan.

When only ten years of age, Solomon had shared his father's flight, and at fifteen he was anointed as his successor. Solomon freely forgave the brother who tried to secure the throne, but when this same young man again tried to be king, he had him put to death.

In this conspiracy perished Shimei, Saul's last descendant, as well as Joab, David's principal captain; and the high priest Abiathar was banished forever. Solomon, having thus secured the throne, now made an alliance with the King of Egypt, and, to strengthen the bond of friendship between them, he married the Pharaoh's daughter.

Shortly after his wedding Solomon went up to the heights of Gibeon, to offer up a great sacrifice. On that selfsame night, he heard the voice of the Lord, bidding him choose any gift he wished, and promising that it should be granted to him.

Solomon was still very young, and he realized that he would need much knowledge to govern his people; so he now asked for wisdom in preference to happiness or wealth. This wish was granted, and because he had thought more of his people's good than of his own, God also promised him long life, riches, and power.

The Great King, for such is the name Solomon bears in Jewish history, soon had occasion to make use of the wisdom that he had obtained. Two women appeared in his judgment hall, clamoring for justice and bringing with them one living and one dead child.

Solomon, with his usual regard for justice, heard both sides of the story; but as both women denied the dead child, and claimed the living, the people present were greatly perplexed. The king, however, seemed to feel no doubts. As both women laid equal claim to the living child, he said that it should at once be cut in two and one half given to each mother.

The guards, in obedience to this order, seized the child, and were about to divide it, when the real mother fell at Solomon's feet, begging him not to injure her child, and offering to give up all right to it, provided it might live.

The other woman, however, stood by unmoved, saying that the judgment was just. By her indifference to the fate of the living child, she showed that the dead one was hers. Solomon, having thus found out the truth, then bade the guards pause. He gave back the child to

THE JUDGMENT OF SOLOMON

the real mother, and received much applause for the way in which he had settled this difficult case.

To extend the kingdom which had been left him by his father, Solomon made alliances with the Kings of Syria and Phœnicia, and greatly increased his riches by trading. In his reign large caravans set out in all directions, and came back from distant climes laden with precious things.

A large fleet of trading vessels also sailed out of Joppa, to bring gold from Ophir, ebony, ivory, spices, precious stones, silken and fine woolen materials, and almost every other thing you can think of. Many of these wares were sold, but the choicest among them were kept for the building or adornment of the great temple, which Solomon wished to erect on Mount Moriah, on the very spot where the angel of pestilence had stood when David was given the choice between a seven years' famine, a three months' flight, or a three days' plague.

CHAPTER XLV

THE BUILDING OF THE TEMPLE

SOLOMON, as we have seen, was very anxious to secure the most precious materials for the building of the temple. He therefore made an agreement with Hiram, King of Tyre, who promised to furnish him huge timbers from the big cedar trees which grew on Mount Lebanon.

These logs were cut and made ready for their future purpose on the spot where they grew, and were then carried to Jerusalem. The stonecutters, in the mean while, had got huge blocks of stone ready for the walls and foundations; and workers in iron, brass, silver, and gold were busy day after day, preparing all that was necessary for the adornment of the costliest edifice that has ever been seen.

We are told that no less than one hundred and eighty thousand men were employed in this work, and the preparation of the material was so complete that no sound of ax or hammer was heard about the building, during the whole seven and a half years needed to finish it.

Solomon, with Hiram his architect, watched this

great edifice slowly rise. It was completed one thousand and five years before Christ, and probably cost more than five billion dollars.

The temple which Solomon thus built had a porch supported by Hiram's masterpieces,—two great brazen pillars. Then came the Holy Place, where stood the altars for incense, the table for the shewbread, and the seven branched golden candlestick; and in the courts were the altar of burnt offering, and a great brazen laver which was called the Sea of Brass. A third inclosure, the Holy of Holies, glittered with gold and precious stones, and within it stood the Ark of the Covenant.

The grandest religious ceremony described in the Old Testament is the dedication of this new temple, which took place at the time of the Feast of Tabernacles, one of the greatest Jewish festivals. People came to Jerusalem from all directions to see it, and although the Promised Land was a small country, no less than five million persons were present at this great ceremony, where God sent down fire from heaven to consume the sacrifice.

Not content with the building of this temple, Solomon also constructed a palace large enough to shelter him, his court, and his seven hundred wives and attendants. The architect Hiram finished it in thirteen years, and hung it around with golden shields which were used for the king's bodyguard.

Within this palace was the great cedar-wood Judgment Hall, where Solomon sat on a marvelous throne of gold and ivory. It was here that he received the Queen of Sheba, who came from afar to visit him, and to find out whether all the tales she had heard of his wealth, power, and wisdom were quite true.

The Queen of Sheba brought Solomon princely gifts, and soon made sure that none of the stories about his wealth and power were exaggerations. Then she satisfied herself about his wisdom by asking him some problems and riddles, which he solved with the greatest ease.

To please his Egyptian wife, Solomon built a second palace, in the mountains, where he and his court spent the warm summer months. But even his royal income of thirty million dollars was not enough to keep up all this magnificence, and to obtain more money Solomon soon had recourse to taxes, which caused the people much suffering, and which in time made them hate him.

As the Israelites could not raise money enough to supply their needs and pay these heavy taxes, they little by little neglected their farming and cattle raising, and began to engage in trade to get larger profits.

Thus they soon came into close contact with many men of different nations, and they learned from them to worship idols, such as were seen in the Syrian and Phœnician temples. Little by little, they thus forgot the Lord their God, who had released them from slavery in Egypt, had given them the Promised Land, and had blessed them with all the prosperity which they now enjoyed.

CHAPTER XLVI

THE DEATH OF SOLOMON

WHEN Solomon had finished all his great works, God renewed to him the promises which had been made to David. He also warned the king that while obedience would be rewarded with great blessings, disobedience would bring about the ruin of both king and people.

Hiram, who had finished the buildings which the king had planned with such magnificence, now went home, after receiving his promised reward of twenty cities, which were all situated in the land of Galilee.

After Hiram had gone, Solomon finished the walls of Jerusalem. Then, to please his foreign wives, he did what he knew was wrong, and set up heathen altars to Ashtoreth and Moloch on the Mount of Olives, directly opposite Mount Moriah, where stood the new temple. Here he not only allowed his wives to offer up sacrifices to the idols, but even helped them to do so.

God had warned him that such disobedience would surely be punished, and as Solomon had worshiped idols he was no longer allowed to enjoy the great prosperity of his early reign. A prophet was therefore sent to Jeroboam, one of Solomon's rivals, to tell him that part of the kingdom would soon be given into his hands.

The prophet met Jeroboam, snatched the new mantle off his shoulders, and tore it into twelve pieces. Then thrusting ten of these into the astonished Jeroboam's hand, he said that God would thus rend the kingdom to pieces, and would give ten tribes into his keeping. This soon came true; ten tribes joined Jeroboam, and the tribe of Judah was the only important one which remained faithful to the royal family. It was left to the king only for the sake of David, and so that the Lord's worship might go on in his temple at Jerusalem.

When Solomon heard this prediction, he tried to bring it to naught by killing Jeroboam; but the intended victim, hearing that his life was in danger, fled into Egypt.

Solomon was haunted all the time by the feeling that his sins had robbed his children of their inheritance. He was also worried by wars with two rivals,—Hadad, Prince of Edom, and Rezon, founder of the kingdom of Damascus; and thus he was very unhappy toward the end of his life.

Solomon was not only one of the greatest kings of the world, but he is also known as a writer. He left three books, which form part of the Old Testament. It is supposed that the first, which is called the Song of Solomon, was written when he was very young; that the second, Proverbs, was the work of his manhood; and that the third and last, Ecclesiastes, was composed in his old age, when he had ceased to take pleasure in anything, and could only say: "Vanity of vanities, all is vanity."

Having found that wealth and wisdom are of no avail to a man who has departed from the ways of the Lord, Solomon died, after a reign of forty years. He had spent all the treasure which his father had left him, and had laid such heavy taxes upon the people that they were poor and oppressed. When he died, he left his son Rehoboam to reap the harvest of dislike which he had sown.

Rehoboam, called to the throne by Solomon's death, went up to Shechem to be proclaimed king. There he was met by Jeroboam, who had now come back from Egypt, and who came to ask him to redress the wrongs under which the oppressed people had suffered so long.

Instead of granting this petition, as all the older men in his council advised him, Rehoboam haughtily refused to reduce the taxes, and said to the people: "My father made your yoke heavy, and I will add to your yoke; my father also chastised you with whips, but I will chastise you with scorpions."

The people, hearing these cruel words, understood that they could expect neither mercy nor justice from the new king, and in their anger they rose up against him. His tax collector was stoned to death, and Rehoboam himself escaped a like fate only by fleeing in his chariot to Jerusalem.

The rebels, left masters of Shechem, now went on to elect Jeroboam king of Israel, and ten of the tribes promised to obey him. Only the tribes of Judah and Benjamin were still faithful to the grandson of David.

To compel the other ten tribes to obey him once more, Rehoboam collected an army of one hundred and eighty thousand men. He was about to march against Jeroboam, when a man of God brought him a divine message, which forbade his going forth to war.

Rehoboam did not dare disobey this order openly, and for many years there was only a pretense of warfare. The two kings, however, were all the time busy in making their armies larger, winning allies, and building strong walls around their towns, so that when the right moment came they could wage war with better chances of success.

CHAPTER XLVII

THE TWO KINGDOMS

THE Chosen People were divided forever. While ten tribes formed the kingdom of Israel, and called Jeroboam their king, the other two formed the kingdom of Judah, and were faithful to Rehoboam.

The adherents of Rehoboam of course went on worshiping in the beautiful new temple which Solomon had built; but those of Jeroboam were not allowed to do so. It seems that this king feared that his subjects, in going up there to sacrifice, might again promise to obey their royal race; so he forbade their worshiping in Jerusalem at all.

To make up to them for this, Jeroboam set up golden calves at Bethel and Dan, although God had forbidden it. He bade the people adore them, and he himself offered up sacrifices and burnt offerings to them. This disobedience was soon and severely punished, as you will see a little farther on.

Although Rehoboam had lost ten tribes at the very outset, the first years of his reign were quite happy, because he tried to be good. But later on he ceased to lead a good life, and allowed his people to fall back into idolatry; and then he was punished sorely. The King of Egypt, an ally of Israel, came into the kingdom of Rehoboam with a large army, took all the strongholds of Judah, and even entered Jerusalem.

The enemy robbed the temple and the palace, and carried off the golden shields which Hiram had made for Solomon's bodyguard, and which were hung all around the king's dwelling. Only a prompt and thorough repentance saved Rehoboam and the people from being carried off into captivity in Egypt at this time.

Besides that, the King of Judah was forced to pay a heavy tribute to the conquerors, but he soon began to repair his losses. The golden shields, among other things, were replaced by like pieces of armor in brass, which, although far less costly, shone quite as brightly as if they had been made of the more precious metal.

Unfortunately, however, neither Rehoboam nor his subjects were faithful for any length of time, and after a reign of seventeen years, this king died and was succeeded by his son Abijah. The new monarch went on waging a petty warfare against the King of Israel. He relied upon the Lord, put down idolatry, and tried to be good, and, therefore, he was rewarded by a victory, and was allowed to become master of three of Jeroboam's towns.

But the virtue of Abijah was not to last long either. He too soon fell into evil ways, and followed the bad example which his father Rehoboam had given him; so his reign was cut short, and Asa, his son, ruled in his stead. At this time the land was in a very promising state, and Asa soon became so strong that the King of Israel feared to attack him, and left him in peace for ten long years.

While Judah had been governed by three kings, Rehoboam, Abijah, and Asa, Israel had been under the sway of the same monarch, Jeroboam. This ruler had established his capital at Shechem, and had been promised that his kingdom would endure if he obeyed the law of God. But this he did not do, for he led his people into idolatry by setting up golden calves at Dan and Bethel.

A prophet came to reprove Jeroboam, and when the king bade his guards seize and put the insolent man to death, none of them dared obey him. As the guards would not lay hands upon the prophet, Jeroboam himself tried to do so; but the arm which he stretched out fell helpless and withered to his side, and an earthquake overthrew the heathen altar which he had just built.

These wonders so frightened the king that he now begged the prophet to pray that his hand might be cured. Then, when this request had been granted, and the arm was well again, Jeroboam humbly asked the Lord's messenger to come into his house and take food.

The prophet had been forbidden to eat or drink there, so he refused the invitation, and started for home. On the way thither, however, he was met by a false prophet, who told him that an angel had come to bid him take food. The true prophet, who was very hungry, now went to the false prophet's house; but even while

THE PROPHET KILLED BY THE LION

he was eating and drinking there he heard the Lord's voice rebuking him for his disobedience.

He was soon punished for listening to the false prophet's lies, for on his homeward journey he was attacked by a lion, which sprang out of a thicket and killed him.

CHAPTER XLVIII

SEVEN KINGS OF ISRAEL

IN spite of all the warnings which he had received, Jeroboam went on in his evil ways. Another punishment, therefore, soon befell him; for he lost his favorite son, the only good member of his family, and the one upon whom rested his greatest hopes.

Then, after a reign of twenty-two years, Jeroboam himself died, leaving the kingdom of Israel to be ruled by his son Nadab.

But as this new ruler led a bad life, he was killed two years later by one of his own captains during a war with the Philistines.

To get the crown, this captain, whose name was Baasha, killed all the other members of the royal family. Thus, by a wholesale murder, he became the third king of Israel, and during his reign of twenty-four years, he followed all the evil ways of the kings who went before him.

He was reproved for his sins and idolatries by a prophet of the Lord, and was punished by a war with

Judah, and one with the King of Syria, who marched into his kingdom and took several of his cities.

Baasha's son Elah was murdered at the end of two years by Zimri, the commander of his chariots, who also killed all the other members of the royal family. But Zimri himself died, a victim of the hatred of his rival, Omri, just seven days after he had come to the throne.

Omri, the sixth king of Israel, is especially noted because, during his short reign of twelve years, he built the city of Samaria, which became the capital of his kingdom. When he died, he left the throne to his son Ahab, the best known of all the kings of Israel.

In the mean while, Asa had reigned quietly over Judah, and, as his "heart was perfect with the Lord all his days," he was allowed to rule forty-one years. During this time Asa rebuilt the walls of Jerusalem, and gathered together a large and well-trained army. As soon as he was all ready, he proudly refused to pay tribute to the Egyptians, although they had forced the people of Judah to make a yearly payment ever since they had entered Jerusalem during the reign of Rehoboam.

The armies of Judah and of Egypt met on the southern border of Palestine, where Asa, in answer to his fervent prayer, was rewarded by a great victory over his foes. When he came back to his capital in triumph, with all the spoil he had won, the people's hearts were full of thanksgiving and joy; so God seized this favorable moment to make a solemn appeal to them through a prophet.

This holy man bade the king and people to be strong, heart and hand, in seeking God, and told them not to worship idols. They were so strongly moved by this speech that they sent away all the idols from their land, and purified their altars. Next they assembled in such large numbers for the worship of the Lord that Baasha, who was then King of Israel, was frightened, and decided to march against them before they could come and attack him.

When Asa heard that the King of Israel was coming to fight him, he quite forgot that he needed no other helper than God, and sought the alliance of the King of Syria. This he managed to get by giving him in exchange all the temple treasures. But a prophet soon came to reprove Asa for this lack of faith in God's help. The prophet told the king that as he had sought the help of a stranger, instead of trusting the Lord, he would have war all the rest of his life.

Asa was so angry when he heard this prophecy that he had the prophet put into prison and persecuted. But he could not forget the words which this unfortunate man had spoken.

Then, too, the prophecy was soon fulfilled, and Asa's last years were made very unhappy by constant warfare and much sickness. He died in the forty-first year of his reign, after having lived long enough to see the first seven kings of Israel.

CHAPTER XLIX

THE GREAT DROUGHT

ASA was succeeded by his son Jehoshaphat, a pious and energetic king, under whose rule the little kingdom of Judah reached its highest point of prosperity. The new king began his reign by pulling down many of the heathen groves and altars, and because he thus tried to stop the worship of idols he was rewarded with great power.

In the course of time, however, Jehoshaphat forgot that God had forbidden his Chosen People to make friends among those who worshiped idols. Not only did he enter into an alliance with Ahab, the idolatrous King of Israel, but he even encouraged his son to marry the daughter of this ruler.

Ahab, the King of Israel with whom the pious Jehoshaphat had thus made an alliance, is known as the greatest, but at the same time the most wicked, of all the rulers of the ten tribes. He began to reign in Samaria while Asa was yet King of Judah, and from the time of his marriage he was completely under the influence of his wife, Jezebel.

This woman is well known as one of the cleverest,

but most wicked, women that ever lived. She brought the worship of the heathen god Baal into her husband's kingdom, set up altars and groves at Samaria, and had no less than eight hundred and fifty heathen priests who were fed at her own table.

Moreover, Jezebel persecuted the prophets of the true God with such fury that they were soon obliged to flee from her, and take refuge in neighboring caves, where they staid hidden. Here they were for a while secretly fed by Ahab's steward, who did not dare to support them openly, because he was afraid of the anger of his haughty mistress.

The Israelites, during the past sixty years, had little by little yielded to the worship of idols, and there were now only seven thousand men among them who had not bent the knee to Jezebel's favorite god, Baal. The Lord, touched by the suffering of these few servants who had thus been faithful to him, now interfered in their behalf.

To help them, he sent Elijah, the greatest prophet since the time of Samuel. Elijah was very tall, his features were rugged and stern, his long hair flowed over his broad shoulders, and he wore a rough robe or mantle of sheep's hair.

Directed by God, this prophet suddenly came to the king's court, where his rough clothes and manners must have made a startling contrast with Ahab's courtiers, who were dressed in costly silks. As soon as he arrived there, he abruptly gave his message: "As the Lord God of Israel liveth, there shall not be dew nor rain these years, but according to my word."

When Ahab heard these words, he shuddered; for, although Jezebel and her priests thought that Elijah was nothing but a madman, Ahab knew very well that he was a prophet of the Lord. Before the astonished king could collect himself enough to bid his guards seize the prophet and put him to death, Elijah had disappeared, and no one could find any trace of him.

The prophet, in leaving the palace, had merely obeyed God's orders. After warning Ahab of the coming drought, he speedily went to a quiet valley far from the houses of men. In this little valley flowed a tiny stream, which emptied its waters into the river Jordan. Here Elijah staid, quenching his thirst in the little stream, and living on the food which the ravens brought to him.

He lived in the valley until the time of the rainy reason came; but, although the ground was very dry, there were no signs of the usually abundant rainfalls. Little by little, even the stream at the bottom of the valley dried up, and then the prophet, in obedience to God's command, left this lonely place and went down into Phœnicia.

Elijah came at last to a village near the seashore, where the famine brought about by the drought was beginning to make itself bitterly felt. Here he saw a poor widow picking up a few sticks to cook her last food; for she had no money, and her whole stock of provisions was a handful of meal and a few drops of oil.

The prophet, whose garments were faded, dusty,

and torn, drew near this woman and asked her for a drink. Then, when his thirst was slaked, he looked up at her with imploring eyes and said: "Bring me, I pray thee, a morsel of bread in thine hand."

Now, although this man was a complete stranger, and although he had come and asked her for what was most precious to her, the woman felt so sorry for him that she led him into her house, and generously shared with him the small amount of food which was all she had to keep herself and her son alive.

In reward for this good deed, the widow was favored by a miracle. During the next three years, which Elijah spent in her house, the meal and oil never failed her, and she and her son and her guest had plenty to eat.

Some time after, the poor woman's son died, and then the prophet further showed how thankful he was for her former kindness, by bringing the boy back to life. This is the very first time in the story of the Bible that we hear of such a miracle as bringing the dead back from the tomb. But, as you will learn from reading the Bible, a like miracle is mentioned several times in the Old, as well as in the New, Testament.

CHAPTER L

THE PRIESTS OF BAAL

IT was only at the end of the third year of drought, that God bade Elijah leave the widow's house and go to Ahab, King of Israel. The prophet did not find the king at his palace, as usual; for Ahab was traveling around the country in search of pasture for his horses, which were suffering sorely from the long drought.

The moment that Elijah appeared, the king remembered his former visit, and, thinking that the prophet was to blame for all the suffering of his people, he angrily cried: "Art thou he that troubleth Israel?"

But Elijah stood fearlessly before the king, and boldly answered:

"I have not troubled Israel, but thou, and thy father's house, in that ye have forsaken the commandments of the Lord, and thou hast followed Baalim."

Then, to show the king the power of God, and to convince him that the idols which he worshiped could really do nothing at all, Elijah invited him to bring all his priests to Mount Carmel. There, he said, the four hundred and fifty priests of Baal might build an altar to their god, while he himself, the only believer in the true God who still dared make his faith known, would erect an altar for Jehovah (the Hebrew name for the Lord).

All the people gathered together on the mountain, where they knew that a test of the powers of God and of Baal was to be made. Then Elijah boldly addressed the multitude, saying: "How long halt ye between two opinions? If the Lord be God, follow him; but if Baal, then follow him."

Next, Elijah went on to say that they would now call upon the true God to make himself known by sending down fire from heaven to burn up the sacrifice laid upon his altar. Not daring to refuse this test, the priests of Baal built their altar, and made use of all their arts, prayers, incantations, and magic, to make Baal hear them.

But the hours passed on without any sign of their prayers being answered. The heathen priests became more and more excited, and danced, and screamed always louder. Elijah, who stood by, watching their antics, mockingly spoke to them from time to time, saying that perhaps their god was out hunting, or that he was talking, sleeping, or away on a journey. He also advised them to make more noise, so that their prayer might be sure to reach Baal's ear.

But when all the efforts of Baal's priests were seen to be vain, and their strength was quite exhausted, Elijah stepped quietly forward and built an altar in his turn. He dug a deep trench all around it, and poured water on his fuel until it was soaked through, and until the ditch around it was full. Then he placed his sacrifice on top of the pile, as usual.

When all was ready, the prophet stood calmly near the altar; and, instead of the wild cries and dances which the priests of Baal had used, he said this simple prayer: "Lord God of Abraham, Isaac, and of Israel, let it be known this day that thou art God in Israel, and that I am thy servant, and that I have done all these things at thy word."

The prayer was scarcely out of his mouth when the fire of heaven came down upon the altar from a cloudless sky, burned up both fuel and sacrifice, and even dried all the water in the trench. When the assembled people saw this miracle, they were afraid, fell down upon their faces, and cried aloud: "The Lord, he is the God."

Elijah now took advantage of the people's admiration for the power of the true God to make them seize the priests of Baal, who were all slain on the very spot where the uselessness of their prayers had been made known.

CHAPTER LI

NABOTH'S VINEYARD

BY the sacrifice upon Mount Carmel Elijah had publicly made known the power and majesty of the God whom he served. When the massacre of the priests of Baal was ended, he turned to Ahab, who had watched all these deeds in awestruck silence, and told him that plenty of rain would soon fall.

This news pleased Ahab so much that he went into his tent to hold a great feast, while Elijah climbed up the mountain, and sat there, his head bowed down upon his knees, in silent prayer. His servant, in the mean time, had orders to watch the sky closely so as to tell him of the first signs of rain.

Six times the servant came back to the place where Elijah was sitting, and reported that the sky was as blue as ever; but the seventh time, he came back, saying: "Behold, there ariseth a little cloud out of the sea, like a man's hand."

This small sign of coming rain was quite enough for Elijah. He now sent word to the king to prepare his chariot and hasten home. The skies quickly grew black with clouds, and the rain fell in torrents, all over the parched and thirsty land, as Ahab drove quickly back to his home at Jezreel, accompanied by Elijah, who ran ahead of him every step of the way.

Arrived at the palace, the story of the day's happenings was told to Jezebel, Ahab's wife, who flew into a terrible rage when she heard that Baal's priests had all been slain. She threatened Elijah, saying: "So let the gods do to me, and more also, if I make not thy life as the life of one of them by to-morrow about this time."

ELIJAH APPEARS BEFORE AHAB

Thus warned that he was in great danger, Elijah managed to escape, followed only by his young servant. They fled without stopping until they had crossed the kingdom of Judah and reached the furthest southern boundary of Palestine.

Then, leaving his servant there, Elijah went on

alone into the wilderness of Sinai, where he sank to the ground, fainting and ready to die. But an angel of the Lord came to him here and touched him on the shoulder. The prophet then looked up and saw a fire, with a cake of bread baked upon it, and near it stood a jar of water.

This food gave Elijah strength enough to spend forty days and forty nights in the wilderness of Sinai. Here he talked with God, whom he was very curious to see. After finding out that the Lord was neither in the wind, nor in the earthquake, nor in the fire, Elijah discovered that he was in the "still small voice," called conscience, which spoke to him, giving him directions as to what he should do next.

Soon after this, Ahab, the King of Israel, wanted to make his palace gardens bigger; so he asked Naboth, a poor man, to give up his vineyard. Naboth was offered a good price for this little piece of land, but he did not wish to sell it. He had inherited it from his father, and, in the eyes of a true Israelite, such a sale was considered a sin.

When Jezebel heard that this poor man had dared to refuse to sell his vineyard to Ahab, she made up her mind to take the little piece of land by fraud, since it could not be obtained by fair means.

At first the queen did not know exactly how to do this, but some one told her that, according to Israelite law, a man who spoke ill of God was punished by being stoned to death, and that his property was given to the king. Jezebel was delighted when she heard this, and she immediately hired false witnesses to say that Naboth had spoken against the Lord.

These men swore before the judges that Naboth was guilty; so Naboth was killed, and the vineyard which the king had longed for became part of the palace garden. But the story of Naboth's death soon became publicly known, and it finally came to the ears of Elijah.

Once more the tall and thin prophet appeared unexpectedly before the eyes of the king; and this time his stern voice was heard proclaiming: "Thus saith the Lord, In the place where dogs licked the blood of Naboth, shall dogs also lick thy blood, even thine. . . . And of Jezebel also spake the Lord, saying, The dogs shall eat Jezebel by the wall of Jezreel." These were awful prophecies, but you will soon see how exactly they were fulfilled.

CHAPTER LII

SEVERAL MIRACLES

A HAB, terrified by the prophecy which Elijah had made about his death, now began to show signs of such deep sorrow that the Lord took pity upon him, and put off for some time the threatened punishment.

Shortly after Elijah's warning, however, Ahab received a visit from his neighbor, Jehoshaphat, King of Judah, and they two began to plan war against the King of Damascus, whom Ahab had already defeated in one war. But Jehoshaphat, who was a godly man, refused to set out until he was sure that the Lord approved of their plan. He therefore asked Ahab's prophets, who all declared that they would win the victory. Only one of these men had the courage to say, what proved to be the truth, that Ahab would lose his life in this war. Although Ahab declared that he did not believe this prediction, he tried to prevent any possible harm by going into battle in disguise. In spite of this caution, he was mortally wounded; but he bravely staid in his chariot until his army gave way, and his panic-stricken soldiers fled, crying: "Every man to his city and every man to his own country."

Before Ahab could reach home, he breathed his last, and his body was buried in his capital, Samaria. But Elijah's prophecy was none the less fulfilled; for the king's blood-stained chariot was washed on the very spot where Naboth had been stoned to death, and the dogs came and licked up his blood.

Ahab was succeeded by his son Ahaziah, who was named king while Jehoshaphat, terrified at the defeat of the forces of Judah and Israel, was hastening back to Jerusalem. During Jehoshaphat's absence from his capital, the tribes of the desert had formed an alliance with the Moabites and Ammonites, and they now soon began to make war against Judah, hoping to throw off the yoke which they had been forced to bear ever since the days of David.

To meet the coming danger in a godly way, Jehoshaphat bade his people fast; then he offered up a sacrifice, and prayed for the help of the Lord. This prayer received a speedy answer; for the spirit of the Lord fell upon one of the Levites, who bade the people go forth on the morrow, and win a victory without striking a blow, their part being merely to stand "and see the salvation of the Lord."

With loud songs of praise the people of Judah marched forth on the next day, and from afar they saw a strange sight. The various nations, confused by the traps and ambuscades which they had set for the men of Judah, had fallen upon each other with fury, and, when Jehoshaphat and his army came up, the ground was all strewn with their dead.

This great deliverance from danger filled the hearts of the Lord's people with joy, and so terrified their enemies that the peace was not again broken as long as Jehoshaphat reigned.

Meanwhile, Ahaziah, the successor of Ahab on the throne of Israel, ruled only two years; but during that short time he imitated all the evil ways of both his parents, and worshiped idols. When he became ill, therefore, his first thought was to send messengers to one of the shrines of Baal. But Elijah met the men on their way thither, and told them that Ahaziah would soon die in punishment for his sins.

When Ahaziah heard that Elijah had dared to speak so, he sent out fifty of his men with orders to seize and kill the prophet. This little troop surrounded Elijah, who was sitting on a hill, and then the captain of the men went up to him, crying: "Thou man of God, the king hath said, 'Come down.'"

In spite of this summons Elijah sat still and answered: "If I be a man of God, then let fire come down from heaven, and consume thee and thy fifty." No sooner had he spoken these words than captain and soldiers perished; and the same fate overtook a second band of soldiers who were told to take him.

When a third troop was sent out by Ahaziah, the frightened captain fell down upon his face before Elijah, begging the prophet to spare him and his men. In obedience to God's command, Elijah then went with the soldiers into the king's presence, where he boldly repeated the words which he had already spoken. This prophecy came true; for Ahaziah, the king, soon died.

CHAPTER LIII

THE CHARIOT OF FIRE

ALTHOUGH Joram, Ahaziah's successor, was not an idolater himself, he allowed Jezebel to go on worshiping Baal, and to lead his people into evil ways. All this king's attention was taken up with wars, in the hope of recovering the land which had fallen into the hands of the King of Damascus.

The hard yoke of Jezebel weighed more and more heavily upon the people of Israel, who, encouraged by their prophets, finally revolted. By God's order one of these holy men sought Jehu, captain of the armies of Israel, anointed him king in Joram's stead, and told him that God was about to cut off the house of Ahab, and put an end to the idolatry in the land.

Jehu made known this divine message to his fellow-officers, who not only joyfully hailed him king, but offered to help him overthrow Joram. They said that the moment seemed very favorable; for the king was ill from a wound which he had received in one of his battles a short time before.

Thus encouraged, Jehu made up his mind to lose no time, and, jumping into his chariot, he drove furiously toward the palace at Jezreel. The king heard that he was coming, and sent a messenger out to meet him and ask what he wanted.

Instead of answering this man, Jehu drove on, and soon saw Joram, the king, who had risen from his bed, and was riding out to meet him. The rebel captain drew his bow, pierced the king with an arrow, and left him dead in the bottom of his chariot.

Having thus killed Joram, Jehu quickly went on to the palace, where Jezebel, who was now sixty years old, but affected the airs and appearance of a young woman, leaned out of the palace window, and taunted him, saying: "What became of Zimri, who murdered his master?"

Instead of answering her, Jehu gave some orders to the servants standing beside her, and they flung her out of the window, down into the court, where Jehu's chariot wheels passed over her body.

In the general confusion caused by this sudden change of rulers, Jezebel's remains were forgotten; so the dogs of the city came upon them and devoured all but her head, hands, and feet; and thus was fulfilled the prophecy which Elijah had made when she unjustly caused the death of poor Naboth.

Jehu now put to death Ahab's seventy sons, all the courtiers, and the priests of Baal. Then after pulling down the temples, altars, and groves which had been consecrated to idols, he restored the worship of the Lord, not only in Samaria, his capital, but throughout his whole kingdom.

In the mean while, the prophet Elijah had been commanded by God to choose Elisha as his successor. Not long after he had done so, he felt that the time was drawing near when his earthly career would be ended; so he journeyed toward Jericho, accompanied by Elisha.

When they came to the banks of the Jordan, Elijah rolled up his mantle, and struck the waters with it, which parted and allowed them both to pass over dry shod. Upon reaching the other side, Elisha asked, as a parting gift, that a double portion of his master's spirit might rest upon him.

Elijah listened to this request in silence, and then promised that it should be granted, provided his disciple were watchful and saw him taken away. The Bible now goes on to say: "And it came to pass, as they still went on and talked, that, behold, there appeared a chariot of fire, and horses of fire, and parted them both asunder; and Elijah went up by a whirlwind into heaven. And Elisha saw it, and he cried: "My father, my father, the chariot of Israel, and the horsemen thereof!"

In this fiery chariot, Elijah the prophet was whirled up out of sight, and as he vanished, his mantle fell down upon Elisha, as a sign that the new prophet's request had been granted. Elisha took up the mantle, and slowly retraced his steps. He tested his power by again dividing the waters of the Jordan with Elijah's cloak; and, going to the prophets at Jericho, he told them all that had occurred.

CHAPTER LIV

NAAMAN THE LEPER

ELISHA had become the successor of Elijah, and it soon became plain that the spirit of the Lord was with him, because he too could work miracles. Among those which we find written in the Book of Kings, we see that he not only divided the waters of the Jordan with Elijah's mantle, but that he also sweetened the waters of a bitter spring at Jericho.

On his way to Bethel, some wicked children once scoffed at him, crying: "Go up, thou bald head!" In punishment for this rude conduct, they were all torn to pieces by the bears that sprang out of the forest upon them.

Elisha next went on to Mount Carmel and to Samaria, where he was openly recognized as a prophet of the Lord. Later on, in the course of his ministry, he multiplied a widow's cruse of oil, so that it filled many jars. These she sold, and the money which she thus got was enough to supply all her needs.

To please a woman who befriended him, Elisha prayed that she might have a son. Five years after this prayer had been granted, the child was taken out into the harvest field by his father. There he was probably overcome by the hot sun, for he sickened and died. When Elisha saw the mother's grief, he felt very sorry for her, and by a miracle brought her dead child back to life.

Elisha once prevented a mess of poisoned pottage from doing any harm to those who ate of it, and at another time he multiplied twenty barley loaves and a few ears of corn so that they were food enough for a famished city. We are also told that he once made an iron ax head to rise to the surface of a stream in which it had fallen, and swim there until it was taken out.

Elisha's most famous miracle was done for the sake of Naaman, a Syrian, who came to him to be cured of his leprosy, which is a terrible disease. The prophet, instead of laying his hands upon him, as Naaman expected, merely bade the man go and wash in the Jordan if he would be clean.

This advice seemed far too simple to please Naaman, and he went off in anger, saying that the rivers in his own country were just as good as all the waters of Israel. As he was thus riding home in high dudgeon, one of his servants spoke to him, and after much persuasion induced him to try the remedy which Elisha had advised, and which he had come so far to obtain.

Naaman then stepped down into the Jordan, and when he had washed, his loathsome disease was all gone, and he was indeed clean. In his delight at being cured, he went back to thank Elisha, and offered him rich gifts, which the prophet refused to accept.

213

Naaman departed; but Elisha's servant secretly followed and stopped him, saying that he had been sent by his master to ask for the gifts. He received them, but instead of being made richer, he was punished for his deceit by suffering all his life from the disease of which Naaman had been cured.

The Syrians, or people of Damascus, ever since they began to wage war against Israel, had been in the habit of making sudden raids into the country to carry off cattle and spoil. Elisha, warned by God of their coming, always sent word to the king, who was thus able to drive the enemy away before they had done any damage. The King of Syria soon heard that the prophet knew all that he said, even in his bedchamber, and that his words were always repeated to the Israelites. He therefore became very anxious to capture Elisha, and sent out an armed force for that express purpose.

The Syrian army surrounded the mountain upon which Elisha had taken refuge, and seemed so large that his poor servant cried out in fear. To reassure him, Elisha fervently prayed that his eyes might be opened; and then the man, looking up, saw the heavenly host mounting guard all around them.

His fear was gone, and when the Syrian army drew near to take Elisha captive, he saw that all the men were struck with sudden blindness. Helpless, and not knowing where to turn, they allowed themselves to be led into the capital of their enemies, where Elisha not only restored their sight, but persuaded the King of Israel to let them go home unharmed.

CHAPTER LV

THE SIEGE OF SAMARIA

THE king, whom Elisha had helped so many times in the war against the Syrians, was Joram. As we have already seen, this ruler of Israel allowed idolatry; and now God withdrew his protection from him, and even permitted the Syrians to march into his kingdom and besiege his capital.

During this siege the people of Samaria suffered much from famine, and at last had nothing to eat but dogs, cats, and mice. We are told that their hunger was so great that some of the inhabitants even became cannibals, and that mothers ate their own children.

The king, who pretended that Elisha was to blame for all these troubles, finally sent for him, intending to cut off his head. But the prophet refused to go to court, and bade the messengers go back and tell the king that there would be plenty of food at Samaria on the morrow. All the Samaritans believed this prophecy except one man, and he was told that, in punishment for his unbelief, he alone would not eat of the promised plenty.

That selfsame day, four lepers went into the Syrian

camp. While they were there, they heard "a noise of chariots and a noise of horses, even the noise of a great host." These sounds caused a panic in the camp, and the Syrians fled in haste, leaving their tents and all their stock of provisions behind them.

After satisfying their own hunger, and securing much plunder, the lepers went and told this news to the king. Then all the people of Samaria swarmed out of the city, and rushed into the deserted camp, where they found plenty to eat. Elisha's prediction was fulfilled in every particular; for the man who had doubted his word was trodden under foot and killed by the hungry multitude as they rushed toward the Syrian camp.

We are told in the Bible that Elisha worked one more miracle, many years after his death. It seems that the gravediggers once hastily flung a body into his grave. As soon as this corpse touched the dead prophet's bones, it came to life again, and the man walked home as if nothing had happened to him.

While Joram was reigning over Israel, another Joram became king of Judah. This man was the son of Jehoshaphat, and had married Athaliah, daughter of Ahab and Jezebel, who influenced him to set up idols.

So great was the wickedness of this king of Judah, we are told, that his reign would have been the last, had not the Lord remembered his covenant with David, and the promise which he had made, that the house of that great king should last.

So, instead of being entirely cut off, Joram, King of Judah, had many troubles. In the first place, several of his cities rose up against him. Then the Philistines and their allies came into his kingdom, plundered his palace, and carried off all his family into captivity, except one son. Last of all, Joram of Judah became very ill, as a prophet had foretold, and died after much suffering, leaving his throne to his son Ahaziah. This young king was so wicked that he was allowed to rule only one year before he too was forced to give up the crown.

You remember, do you not, how Joram, King of Israel, was killed by his captain, Jehu? Well, at that time, Ahaziah of Judah was on a visit to the King of Israel, and rode out of the city with him on the day of his death. When Joram was shot, Ahaziah fled, but he too had been struck by one of Jehu's arrows, and soon died.

It was not enough to have killed two kings and one queen, so Jehu slew also many other members of the royal house of Israel. In fact, only one member of Ahab's family was now left. This was Athaliah, the mother of Ahaziah, King of Judah. As soon as Athaliah heard that her son was dead, she treacherously killed, as she thought, all her children and grandchildren, so that she might wield the royal scepter herself, and keep up the worship of Baal in Judah.

But her grandson Joash, the son of Ahaziah, was saved by his nurses, who carried him, bleeding and almost lifeless, to his aunt, the wife of the high priest. She gladly received this little charge, and brought him up in the temple in secret.

Joash himself did not know who he really was, and Athaliah was allowed to reign over Judah undisturbed for more than six years. But in the seventh year, a conspiracy was formed by the high priest, and Joash was proclaimed king in the temple.

The priests, armed with the sacred weapons, stood around the child king, ready to defend him, when Athaliah suddenly burst into the temple. She had heard rumors of an uprising, and came there to put it down with a high hand. When she saw her own grandson seated upon the throne, and heard the joyful shouts of the people, she would have liked to flee.

But it was too late. The measure of her crimes was full, and the priests killed her just as she was about to escape. Many of her followers were also slain, and the heathen idols which she had worshiped were banished from the kingdom.

CHAPTER LVI

JOASH KING OF JUDAH

THE new king, Joash, was only seven years old, so the high priest ruled in his stead, and under his wise management, "all the people of the land rejoiced." It now seemed that with two such kings as Joash and Jehu, the kingdoms of Judah and Israel must long prosper; but, as we shall see, their happiness soon came to an end.

Jehu was the first to relax his efforts to reform his people, and when he too finally sank into idolatry, he was made to suffer for his sins by the King of Syria, who invaded his realm. When Jehu died, he was succeeded by his son Jehoahaz. This king also sinned, and for this reason he was forced to fight against Syria throughout his reign of seventeen years.

During this time, the kingdom of Judah prospered under the rule of Joash. Advised by the high priest, this king not only destroyed all the idols, but he undertook to repair the temple, and to make new vessels for it to replace those which Athaliah had taken for the service of Baal. All the people were asked to give money for this purpose, and, so that none should know how much each man gave, the king made the first money chest, which was placed at the gate of the temple. There was a slit in the cover of this box, which was opened every day, when the money was counted and given over to the man who had charge of the repairs.

Joash reigned forty years, and as long as he kept the religion of his fathers, the kingdom prospered; but when he began to worship idols, trouble came. Zechariah, his foster brother, who was now high priest, once scolded Joash for worshiping idols. This reproof made the king so angry that he had the priest stoned to death, although he had once loved him dearly.

In punishment for this crime, the Lord now allowed the King of Syria to come into Jerusalem, and carry away the treasures of the palace and temple. The enemy caused much suffering to the people of Judah, who were angry at Joash for bringing them such misfortune. Some of them even forgot that he was their king, and allowed his own servants to murder him after the Syrians were gone.

Joash was succeeded by his son Amaziah, who, on the whole, was a just king. He punished the men who had murdered his father, but spared their families. This was a very unusual act of mercy at that time; for generally when a man did wrong his family suffered too.

When about to make war against the Edomites, Amaziah hired some Israelite soldiers, so as to make his army larger. But a prophet warned him not to keep them; so he sent these men away, and, with only his own troops, defeated the enemy and took their capital.

But although Amaziah had obeyed the prophet once, he soon disobeyed him by offering up a sacrifice to the principal idol of the Edomites. Because he did this, he had much trouble, and finally fell into the hands of the King of Israel, who was named Joash, like Amaziah's father.

Joash of Israel not only took Amaziah prisoner, but marched into Jerusalem through a breach in the wall. Then, when he had taken all the treasures from the temple and palace, he allowed Amaziah to continue reigning, which he did for the next fifteen years. At the end of that time, his people had learned to hate him so greatly that they killed him after he had fled in terror from his capital.

Meanwhile, after the death of Jehu, the kingdom of Israel had been governed by Jehoahaz and the Joash who took Jerusalem, as we have just seen. Hearing that Elisha was very ill, this king once went to visit him. When he saw that the prophet was about to die, he began to weep bitterly; but Elisha paid no attention to his tears, and told him to take his bow and arrows.

Laying his dying hand upon Joash's hand, Elisha bade him shoot an arrow out of the window. Then, after the king had struck the ground three times with an arrow, the prophet told him that he would win as many victories over the Syrians. This prophecy came true, and it was only after he had won several cities that Joash died, and his son Jeroboam II. began to reign over the ten tribes.

This Jeroboam was the thirteenth king of Israel, and during his long reign of forty-one years, his people were very happy. He won for them all the land east of the Jordan which was in the hands of the Syrians, and even went to attack the great city Damascus.

CHAPTER LVII

THE STORY OF JONAH

IT was probably under the reign of Jeroboam II., one of the greatest kings of Israel, that the word of the Lord came to Jonah, the prophet, saying: "Arise, go to Nineveh, that great city, and cry against it; for their wickedness is come up before me."

When Jonah heard these words, he was terrified; for Nineveh was not only the great city of Assyria, but one of the finest towns of the ancient world. It lay far to the northeast of Palestine, and was under the rule of a powerful and very despotic race of kings, who took pleasure in building some of the most remarkable edifices in the world.

Although more than twenty-five hundred years have passed since the kingdom of Assyria was destroyed, explorers have lately found the ruins of this great city. After digging in huge mounds of rubbish, they found ruined palaces, adorned with wonderful paintings and sculptures, many of which have been carried to the European museums.

At the time when the voice of the Lord came to Jonah, Nineveh had reached the highest point of its glory and prosperity. The prophet knew the pride of the people, and the power of the king; and it is no wonder that he did not care to go there to deliver so disagreeable a message.

In his terror, Jonah fled to the seaport of Joppa, where he went on board a ship bound for Tarshish. His object was to get as far away from Nineveh as possible, so that he would not need to do as the Lord had bidden him. But no sooner were they far out at sea than a terrible storm arose, endangering the vessel and the lives of all on board.

The sailors, according to the custom of the time, declared that there must be some guilty person on the ship, whose presence brought this peril upon them all. To discover the culprit, they drew lots, and when Jonah was thus found to be the sinner, they cast him overboard, "and the sea ceased from her raging. . . . Now the Lord had prepared a great fish to swallow up Jonah; and Jonah was in the belly of the fish three days and three nights."

We are further told that Jonah, who was still alive, "prayed unto the Lord his God out of the fish's belly," and that God had pity upon him and bade the fish vomit Jonah out upon dry land.

The prophet had been saved from great peril by a miracle, and when the Lord again bade him go to Nineveh, he no longer dared disobey. He finally reached the city, which was so large that it took several days to walk around it. Jonah viewed its magnificent buildings and beautiful sculptures, and, standing perhaps near

JONAH

one of the colossal statues which have been found in the ruins, he preached repentance to the people, threatening them with the overthrow of their great city within forty days, if they refused to listen to his words.

It seems that the people of Nineveh believed God's words and led better lives. And, because they "turned from their evil way, . . . God repented of the evil that he had said that he would do unto them; and he did it not."

Of course the men of Nineveh were overjoyed to escape the threatened punishment, but Jonah, the prophet, was disappointed because the judgment of God was staid. He went outside the city, and sat there in sulky silence, under a little booth over which the Lord caused a gourd vine to grow in the course of a single night.

The cool shade of the spreading vine was very grateful to the angry prophet, during the sunny hours of an eastern day. But the next night a worm came and gnawed the roots, so that the vine died. Jonah, deprived of its shelter, now complained aloud.

In answer to his murmurs, God said: "Thou hast had pity on the gourd, for the which thou hast not labored, neither madest it grow; which came up in a night, and perished in a night. And should not I spare Nineveh, that great city, wherein are more than six score thousand persons that cannot discern between their right hand and their left?"

You see, it was for the sake of the innocent little children, who could not tell their right hand from their left, that God had spared the great city; and he now wished to remind Jonah that one should be far more pitiful toward one's fellow-creatures than toward a mere plant.

CHAPTER LVIII

THE CAPTIVITY OF ISRAEL

UNDER the reign of Jeroboam II., or of the kings who came just before, two other prophets arose in Israel, Hosea and Amos. Both spoke prophecies which are written down in the Bible, in books bearing their names. Hosea foretold the captivity of his people, and their return to the Holy Land, and he compared the sins of the people to those of his own wife, who had forsaken him. The Lord's forgiveness of his people was further made clear by Hosea's own generosity in receiving again, and tenderly supporting, this runaway wife in her old age.

Amos, the other prophet, was called from his labors as a shepherd to speak against idolatry, and to foretell the doom of all the nations that dwelt in that part of Asia. He too foretold the return from captivity, and before he died he had visions concerning the coming of the Messiah.

After reigning forty-one years, Jeroboam II., King of Israel, was succeeded by his son, who indulged in sin, and fell under the blows of a conspirator. This man destroyed all that was left of the race of Jehu, and took possession of the throne. But he did not long enjoy the royal authority; for he was murdered one month later by Menahem, who became king and reigned ten years, treating the people with great cruelty.

It was under the reign of Menahem, and while he and his people were again worshiping idols, that the strong Assyrians first came to attack the kingdom. But the king managed to buy them off, by offering them one thousand talents of silver to leave Israel in peace.

The second king after Menahem, however, made an alliance with the Syrians, and, thus strengthened, dared to fight against the haughty Assyrians. He was defeated, and saw a large part of his people led off into captivity, as had been foretold by the prophets. Menahem himself was allowed to keep his poor kingdom, but was soon murdered by Hoshea, his successor, the nineteenth and last king of Israel.

While all these unfortunate events were taking place in the kingdom of Israel, Amaziah, King of Judah, had been succeeded by his son Uzziah, an able monarch. As Uzziah served the Lord, he was granted a long and prosperous reign. But, encouraged by prosperity, he finally became very proud, and forgot to whom his blessings were due. He tried to assume the duties of a priest, which the Levites alone were allowed to perform; and thus he called forth the wrath of God.

Uzziah came into the temple to burn incense, in spite of the high priest and of eighty of his assistants; but as soon as he began it, the Lord struck him with leprosy, and a white plague spot suddenly appeared on his forehead.

When the people saw what had happened, they all took up the cry of "unclean, unclean," and drove Uzziah out of the temple, which his presence polluted. He had to go away to a lonely place, where he spent the rest of his life in torture, while his son governed in his name.

When Uzziah finally died, his son Jotham became king, and for sixteen years he ruled over Judah in the fear of the Lord, and led a godly and faultless life. But in spite of all his virtues, the people gradually grew more corrupt; and when Ahaz, his son, succeeded him, and no longer tried to restrain them, they again openly worshiped idols.

To punish Ahaz for thus sinking with his people into such gross idolatry, the Lord allowed the Kings of Israel and Syria to defeat him in war, and to kill one hundred and twenty thousand of his men. Jerusalem would have fallen into the hands of the Israelites on this occasion, had not Isaiah, a prophet, encouraged the people to repent and defend themselves bravely against the attack.

Thus delivered from the danger of falling into the enemy's hands, Ahaz still had to war against the Syrians and Philistines, who had both attacked him. But instead of relying upon the help of the Lord, Ahaz called the Assyrians to his aid, offering all the temple treasure as a bribe, and promising to recognize the Assyrian king as his lord.

In answer to this appeal, the Assyrians marched

against Damascus, killed the Syrian king, and carried his people off into captivity. It was then, as we have seen, that a part of the Israelites were also captured and led away. They were the tribes of Reuben, Gad, and Manasseh, the very ones who had claimed the land east of the Jordan.

Ahaz then went to Damascus and had a talk with the Assyrian king, to whom he gave the sacred golden vessels, the bases under the lavers, and many other of the priceless ornaments of the temple. The King of Judah had by this time grown so wicked that he set up a heathen altar in the temple; and he would probably have done much more harm, had not his reign been mercifully cut short.

CHAPTER LIX

THE STORY OF TOBIT

THE wicked King of Judah, Ahaz, was succeeded by Hezekiah, his son, who "did that which was right in the sight of the Lord." He reopened and purified the temple, restored the worship of God, and called the people together to celebrate a grand Passover, the first which is mentioned since the time of Joshua.

On this solemn occasion, Hezekiah, the good king, publicly asked God's pardon for all who had sinned; and he pulled down all the heathen idols and altars. He even ordered that the Brazen Serpent, which had been made by Moses, should be broken to pieces, because the people had now begun to worship this too.

Then, relying upon the help of the Lord, Hezekiah drove back the Philistines, and boldly refused to pay any more tribute to the Assyrians. Of course they were very angry when they heard that this Jewish king had thus tried to free himself from their power, and they soon came marching toward Palestine.

Hoshea, King of Israel at that time, followed Hezekiah's example; so the Assyrians came into his land, and made his people suffer so much that they were glad to get rid of the enemy by promising to pay the tribute. Not long after this, however, the Israelites revolted again, and this time the Assyrians besieged Samaria. They became masters of this city after a three years' siege, and carried off twenty-seven thousand, two hundred and eighty families into captivity.

Thus the kingdom of Israel came to an end, and the ten tribes which formed it were led away to Assyria, whence they never came back as a separate people.

As you know, there are many different kinds of churches; well, there are different kinds of Bibles, too. In some of them nothing more is said about the ten tribes, but in the others we are told that some of the captives went on worshiping God in their new homes. In these Bibles also we find the story of Tobit, which is so interesting that many pictures have been made of the scenes which it describes.

The story tells that Tobit, a good Israelite, lent all his money to his poorer brethren, until he had none left, and had to depend on his daily labor for bread. One day, during the noon hour, he lay down in the shadow of a wall to sleep.

Some birds, building their nest above him, let fall little pieces of lime, which dropped into Tobit's eyes and made him lose his sight. Blind now, and unable to work, Tobit called his young son Tobias, bidding him seek a guide, and journey to a distant province. Here the young man was to find an old friend of his father's, and collect from him a sum of money, loaned many years before.

Young Tobias found a guide at the city gates, and set out with him, not knowing that he was the angel Raphael in disguise. In the course of their journey, Tobias, while bathing in a river, was attacked by a monster fish. Helped by the angel, he not only escaped from all peril but also caught the fish. After taking the gall and gills, which by the angel's advice he carried with him, Tobias went on.

He finally reached the debtor's house, and not only collected the sum of money, but also married the man's daughter. This damsel had already been married seven times, but each one of her husbands had been killed on his wedding night by a demon who loved her.

By the angel's advice, Tobias burned the fish gills in the wedding chamber, and the smoke killed the jealous demon. Then Tobias joyfully went home, with his bride and with the money which he had gone to seek.

The angel Raphael, who had ever been at his side, now bade Tobias rub his father's eyes with the fish gall. Thus the pious old man got back his sight just in time to see the heavenly messenger resume his angelic form, and wing his way back to heaven, amid the adoring silence of the happy family whom he had befriended.

TOBIAS AND THE ANGEL

CHAPTER LX

THE ASSYRIAN HOST

AFTER the siege of Samaria, the Assyrian host began to besiege the city of Tyre, which held out bravely for five years. But before it could be taken, the Assyrians were called home by a war with the Medes and Babylonians, and the Tyrians fancied that they had won.

But Isaiah, the great prophet whose predictions are written in the Bible, in a book bearing his name, sadly warned the merchant city of Tyre that although she had escaped this time, she was doomed to utter destruction.

Soon after this, Hezekiah, King of Judah, was "sick unto death." He was very unwilling to die, and in his distress he sent for Isaiah, begging the prophet to make his life longer. Isaiah then promised the king that he should get well again, and in token of the truth of this promise, the prophet made the shadow creep back ten degrees on the sundial, and said that Hezekiah's life would be lengthened by fifteen years.

This respite, and the miracle of the sundial, came to the ears of the King of Babylon; so he sent an embassy to congratulate Hezekiah, and to offer to make an alliance with him against Assyria. Hezekiah was so proud to receive an embassy from the Babylonian king that he showed all his wealth to the messengers, and even let them see all the treasures of the temple.

Isaiah was indignant at this vain display, and sadly told Hezekiah that his treasures would be wrested away from him, not by the Assyrians, whom he feared, but by the Babylonians, whom he trusted. Now that they knew what wealth was there, he said, they would long to get it.

When Hezekiah heard this, he repented of his vanity, and humbled himself before the Lord. He prayed so fervently for forgiveness that he was told that the misfortunes which had been foretold would not be allowed to happen during his day.

The Assyrian king, having made peace at home, again came into Judah, on his way to conquer Egypt. And now, although Isaiah had foretold the downfall of the Egyptians, the Jews offered them their alliance.

The Egyptians, sure of their own strength, scornfully refused to receive any help, and all that the Jews gained by their rash behavior was to call down upon their own heads the wrath of the Assyrians. Isaiah bitterly reproached his countrymen for what they had done, but at the same time he told them they need not fear the Assyrians, because God would defeat the invaders by strange means, while the people need but stand by and see his power.

Reassured by these words, Hezekiah at first showed

no fear when the Assyrians came, but later on, influenced by the terrified people, he tried to buy off the invaders, by giving them three hundred talents of silver and thirty talents of gold. This large sum was procured by the sacrifice of his own plate, and by stripping the precious metal off the temple pillars.

The Assyrian king nevertheless sent one of his generals to take possession of Jerusalem, and then Isaiah's prophecy was fulfilled; for, in the dead of night, "the angel of the Lord went out, and smote in the camp of the Assyrians a hundred four score and five thousand." When the Jewish watchman looked out in the early morning, he saw all the plain strewn with corpses!

Hezekiah, thus saved by a miracle from the awful danger which threatened him, now spent the rest of his life in peace and prosperity, and when he died he was honored by the chief place in the sepulcher of the Kings of Judah.

He was succeeded by Manasseh, his son, who was then only twelve years of age, and who ruled over the country fifty-five years. In the first part of this long reign, Manasseh fell into idolatry, profaned the temple, and made his own son undergo a heathen rite, and "pass through the fire," a sacrifice to Moloch.

Manasseh dealt with wizards and witches; he persecuted many of the prophets, and probably killed Isaiah. It was in punishment for all these sins that the Assyrians were again allowed to come into his kingdom, and even to carry him off into captivity.

Then Manasseh felt so sorry for all the wrong he

had done that God took pity upon him, and sent him back to his kingdom at Jerusalem. Here this king spent the rest of his life quite comfortably; and when he died he left his throne to his son Amon.

CHAPTER LXI

THE PROPHECIES OF JEREMIAH

A S Amon, the new King of Judah, was wicked and idolatrous, his reign lasted only two years, and he died the victim of a conspiracy. His son Josiah succeeded him, and reigned at Jerusalem thirty-one years. This king was a very virtuous man, and although the people all around him were terribly wicked, he remained good and chose to serve the Lord.

At twenty years of age, Josiah made a journey all through his kingdom, asking his people to put away idolatry, destroying their idols, and collecting money to repair the temple. It was at this time that the high priest again found the long-lost and nearly forgotten book of the law, and read it aloud to the king.

Josiah was so impressed when he heard the terrible punishments threatened that he tore his clothing, and called for a prophet to come and explain to him the parts he could not understand. But all the prophets had been killed, and it was only after long search that a woman was found who could tell him the meaning of the sacred words.

She said that all that was written was true, but

comforted the mourning king by telling him that he should not see the downfall of Jerusalem. To save his people if possible, Josiah ordered a public reading of the law, pulled down all the idols that were left, and defiled Tophet, the hot fire kindled for the worship of Moloch.

When Jerusalem had been thoroughly purified, he put all the wizards and witches to death, and then celebrated the Passover at Jerusalem, according to the teachings of the newly found book of the law.

While all these changes were taking place in Judah, the strong Assyrian kingdom had fallen into the hands of the Babylonians and Medes; and Nineveh, the proud city, was destroyed as had been foretold by Isaiah and two lesser prophets.

Hearing that the Egyptians were on their way to attack the Babylonians, his allies, Josiah made an attempt to stop them. In this battle, however, he received a mortal wound, and he died almost as soon as he reached Jerusalem. His death was mourned by the great prophet Jeremiah, and by all the people.

Josiah was the sixteenth and last real king of Judah; for although four others bore that name, they were only the servants of the Egyptian or Babylonian kings, who ruled the people and country as they pleased.

The Egyptians, angry because Josiah had tried to stop them, came to attack Jerusalem under his successor. After pulling him down from the throne, they named his brother Jehoiakim king in his stead. This new king did evil, so Jeremiah rebuked him in the name of the

Lord, and again foretold that the Jews would be taken in captivity to Babylon, whence they would return only after many years.

The king vainly tried to silence the prophet, but Jeremiah went on to foretell the destruction of the temple. This prediction so enraged the priests that they would have put him to death, had not the judges declared that a prophet had the right to say anything he pleased.

By this time the Babylonians had fought and defeated the Egyptians, and marching into Palestine, they now laid siege to Jerusalem, and took the city after a short resistance. Jehoiakim was allowed to keep the throne, on condition that he would be the vassal of Babylon; and the conquerors departed, carrying off all the vessels of the temple, and a number of noble Hebrew youths, who were to be detained at their court as hostages.

Jerusalem was left in a very sorry condition, and the humbled people kept a solemn fast, during which Jeremiah again begged them to turn from their evil ways and repent. With the help of an assistant, Jeremiah wrote down all the prophecies he had uttered, and he now ordered that they should be read aloud, so that the people might see that some of them had already been fulfilled.

Jehoiakim, the king, was not present at this solemn reading, but he sent a man to get the prophecies and read them to him. He was so displeased, however, with what he heard that he burned the roll as soon as it was read. This proved to be of no use, for, by the Lord's command, Jeremiah again made his assistant write down every word he had said, adding a prophecy about the desolation which was to happen to Judah, and about the king's disgraceful end.

CHAPTER LXII

THE CAPTIVITY OF JUDAH

JEHOIAKIM relied upon the help of the Egyptians, and soon revolted against Nebuchadnezzar, King of Babylon. This king was busy just then with another war, so he paid no heed at first to the uprising of the Jews.

When the war was ended he marched against Jerusalem, and put Jehoiakim to death in the way that Jeremiah had foretold. The son of Jehoiakim now became King of Judah, but, as he was only eight years of age, his courtiers reigned in his stead. They were neither good nor wise, and made so much trouble that Nebuchadnezzar, in anger, came again to Jerusalem, and carried off the king, his courtiers, and ten thousand prisoners.

It was probably some time during these campaigns that an event took place which you will not find in some Bibles, but which you will often see in pictures. It seems that one of the Assyrian generals caused so much trouble in the country, that a brave Jewish woman named Judith made up her mind to kill him. She dressed herself up in her finest clothes, and went down to the general's tent, pretending that she had come to visit him because she

JUDITH

loved him. The general gave her a grand supper, and when he fell asleep after drinking much wine, she took a sword and cut off his head. Then she called her servant, put the dead general's head in a cloth, and carried it home, to show her people what she had done.

As Jerusalem could not be left without a ruler, the Babylonians now chose Zedekiah, Josiah's youngest son, to fill this office. He was a vassal of Nebuchadnezzar, and as he closely followed Jeremiah's advice during the beginning of his reign, all went well at first.

Made bold by success, Zedekiah fancied that he might shake off the Babylonian yoke, so he sought the alliance of Egypt. In punishment, his capital was again besieged, and at the end of two and a half years it fell into the hands of the Babylonians. They took Zedekiah captive and sacked the city of Jerusalem.

Not only were the temple and the houses burned, but the city walls were all torn down. This calamity seemed so great to the Jews that the anniversary of this evil day was always observed as a time of mourning and fasting.

Although the Babylonians would have liked to carry all the population off into captivity, the people had suffered so much during the long siege that only eight hundred and thirty-two of them were strong enough to stand the long journey.

The others were left in Palestine, to farm the land and take care of the vineyards. The country was placed under the rule of a governor, advised by Jeremiah. The prophet told the people to be patient and to submit, and at first they were so weak and so tired of war that they were only too ready to obey; but as soon as they got back strength, they again revolted, choosing a prince of Jewish blood as their leader.

After murdering the governor whom Nebuchadnezzar had given them, the Jews suddenly began to fear the wrath of the Babylonians. Hoping to escape from it, they fled into Egypt, where they fancied that they would be safe, although Jeremiah warned them that Egypt also would soon fall into the hands of Nebuchadnezzar.

This prophecy was also spoken at the same time by Ezekiel, who was among the captive Jews at Babylon. It came true, too, before long; for Nebuchadnezzar became master of Tyre, after a siege of more than thirteen years, and then went on to conquer Egypt.

The Jews who had taken refuge in Egypt were duly punished, and when the Babylonian army went home, they took with them long caravans of captives, and left Judah a desert. These captives found many of their friends at Babylon, for twice before some of the Jews had been led thither into bondage.

CHAPTER LXIII

NEBUCHADNEZZAR'S DREAMS

THE young Jewish hostages whom Nebuchadnezzar had carried off in the beginning of his reign, had grown up in Babylon, where they had received their education. But although so far away from home, and completely cut off from their people, they had not forgotten that they belonged to God's Chosen Race.

A few among them, following the example of Daniel, their young chief, ate pulse rather than defile themselves with the meat upon the king's table, which had first been placed on the altars of the idols. One of the officers in charge, seeing the young men eat such poor food, tried to force them to partake of better fare, lest they should grow thin and weak, or starve to death.

But Daniel coaxed this man to let them go on eating pulse, and when the officer saw that the young captives were ruddier and stronger than their companions, he no longer troubled them. We are told in the Bible that God gave all these Hebrew youths much knowledge, but that to Daniel, his servant and prophet, he gave a keen insight into dreams and visions, a power which was to prove very useful.

In the second year of his reign, Nebuchadnezzar was greatly worried by a dream which came every night, but which he could never remember when he awoke. He asked the wise men to describe this dream to him and to explain its meaning; but all in vain. Now, Nebuchadnezzar was in the habit of always having his own way; and when these men did not answer him he was so angry that he wanted to put them all to death. But Daniel came and begged the king not to do so, saying that he would tell and explain the vision in their stead.

After a short prayer, in which he asked the help of the Lord, Daniel came back and told the king that he had seen in his dreams a great statue, with a golden head, silver arms and breast, brazen belly and thighs, iron legs, and feet and toes that were part iron and part clay. This statue was knocked down by a stone,— cut without hands from the living rock,—which came rolling along with great force. Then, having broken the image into pieces, this stone grew larger and larger, until it became a great mountain which filled all the earth.

Next, Daniel told the meaning of this strange dream. He said that the different parts of the statue represented different kingdoms. The head of gold was the kingdom of Babylon. Then would come in turn other powers which would be like the silver, brass, iron, and clay. But all these kingdoms would come to an end, when "the God of heaven set up a kingdom which shall never be destroyed."

Like a great many of the prophecies, this was not

understood until many years after, but now we are told that the golden head stood for the kingdom of the Assyrians and Babylonians, and the silver arms and breast for the Medes and Persians, who next took possession of Babylon. The brazen belly and thighs were the kingdom founded by Alexander the Great; the iron legs stood for the Roman Empire, and the iron and clay feet and toes represented the many but short-lived kingdoms which were formed from it. Finally, the Christians say that the stone, cut without hands from the living rock, was to represent the religion taught by Jesus Christ, which would in time spread all over the face of the earth.

Nebuchadnezzar was so astonished that Daniel could describe and explain his dream, that he fell down upon his face at the young prophet's feet, and did homage to him. In reward for this service, he made Daniel ruler over the whole province of Babylon, and gave important offices to his three companions.

Although the king knew that God had helped Daniel, he would not yield to the Lord, but soon afterwards set up a golden image which he bade all his subjects worship; and when the three young Jews whom he had so highly honored, refused to bow down before it, he condemned them to be cast into a fiery furnace.

This mode of execution had already often been tried, even on the Jews, and all the victims had died. Imagine Nebuchadnezzar's surprise, therefore, when he saw the youths calmly walking about amid the flames, in company with a fourth figure, which looked like an angel.

The king at once ordered that the young men should be set free, and they came out of the fiery furnace unharmed, and even without any odor of fire about their hair or garments. But in spite of this miracle, the king did not yet believe fully in the power of the God of the Jews.

Shortly after, Nebuchadnezzar was greatly troubled by another vision, or dream, in which he saw a great tree which overshadowed all the earth. But even while he was admiring it, he heard a voice from heaven order that the tree should be cut down, and that his man's heart should be changed into that of a beast for seven years' space.

None of the wise men could explain this dream, so Daniel was again called upon. The young Hebrew prophet told Nebuchadnezzar that the mighty tree stood for him, that he would be cut down in his pride, and that for the space of seven long years his reason would forsake him, and he would eat grass like the beasts of the field.

Although Daniel warned Nebuchadnezzar that this calamity could be warded off only by repentance, the King of Babylon went on living as before. One year later the prophecy came true; the mighty king became insane, and for seven years he was like the "beasts of the field."

Nebuchadnezzar, however, recovered his reason at the end of the appointed time, and, doing honor to

God, went on reigning over Babylon for many years. His career was brilliant to its end, and when he died, his son succeeded him.

CHAPTER LXIV

THE FEAST OF BELSHAZZAR

THE new ruler of Babylon seems to have been a very kind monarch; for he took Jehoiachin, the King of Judah, out of his prison. Although this captive was not allowed to return to Jerusalem, he was treated like a guest in the Babylonian palace. We know but little of this King of Babylon, but we are told that he was soon followed by Belshazzar.

Many great changes had been brought about in the Eastern world in the mean while. The Median empire, which had taken the place of the mighty Assyrian realm, was now in its turn to be conquered by a king of Persia called Cyrus the Great. He is called in the Bible the "anointed of the Lord," because he was the man chosen to fulfill some of the old prophecies.

As soon as Cyrus became master of Persia, Media, and Assyria, he longed also to conquer the more southern province of Babylon, and secretly made plans to enter into the city when his coming was not expected, and take possession of it.

One night, Belshazzar and all his courtiers were feasting in one of the magnificent palace halls. The king, probably excited by the wine he had drunk, suddenly gave orders that the golden vessels taken from the temple at Jerusalem should be brought to grace his feast.

He was just drinking out of one of these sacred cups, when all at once a ghostly hand appeared before him, and traced on the palace wall three mysterious words which he could not understand. Belshazzar grew pale and trembled, and sent in haste for the wise men; but they could not explain what the words meant.

Then the queen remembered that Daniel had explained Nebuchadnezzar's visions, and by her advice he was brought into the banquet hall. Without a moment's hesitation, the prophet of the Lord boldly told Belshazzar that because he had not humbled his heart before God he was about to be punished.

The mysterious words, "Mene, mene, tekel, upharsin," he said, meant that God had weighed Belshazzar in the balance and found him wanting, and that his kingdom would now be taken from him and given to the Persians.

Belshazzar rewarded Daniel for his explanation, which he either did not believe or tried to forget by going on with the feast. But that very night, when the revelers were fast asleep, the Persians secretly entered Babylon by turning aside the river which passed through it, and noiselessly following its bed into the very heart of the city.

In the Bible, we are simply told that "in that night was Belshazzar, the King of the Chaldeans, slain." Cyrus was now King of Babylon, but he spared the Jews in the general massacre which took place. Then, while the Persian king went on with his wars, Darius, the Mede, governed the conquered city, with the help of Daniel, who had been a faithful servant of the former kings.

Now it seems that many of the court officers were greatly offended at being obliged to render account to a Jew, and sought an excuse to get rid of Daniel. It was hopeless, they knew, to wait for him to commit any fault, so they made a plot whereby his religion would bring him into trouble with Darius.

Prompted by these artful men, Darius made one of those very strict laws, which even a king could not change, and said that no one should address any prayer to God or man for thirty days, under penalty of being cast into the lions' den.

Although Daniel knew this order, he did not let it hinder him. Opening his window, as usual, toward Jerusalem, he offered up his daily prayers. His enemies, lying in wait, found him out and told Darius; and then the king, although he would have liked to spare Daniel, was forced to keep his own law, and ordered that the prophet should be cast into the lions' den.

Darius, however, must have believed that God had the power to protect his servant; for he said to Daniel: "Thy God whom thou servest continually, he will deliver thee." It seems that Darius did not fear the hungry lions so much as he did his wicked courtiers; for as soon as his orders had been obeyed, he had a stone placed over the opening of the den, and set his seal upon it, so that it could not be moved without his knowledge.

Early on the next day, Darius hastened to the lions' den, and had the stone pushed aside. Then, bending over the dark hole, he anxiously cried: "O Daniel, servant of the living God, is thy God, whom thou servest continually, able to deliver thee from the lions?"

From the depths of that awful den came the calm reply: "My God hath sent his angel, and hath shut the lions' mouths, that they have not hurt me." Daniel was now set free, his accusers were hurled into the lions' den in his stead, and Darius said publicly that Daniel's God should be honored throughout all the land.

DANIEL IN THE LIONS' DEN

CHAPTER LXV

THE RETURN FROM CAPTIVITY

THERE is a story told about Daniel which is not found in all Bibles, but which has so often been used as a subject for pictures that it should be well known. This story tells us that when Daniel was very young, he was once present where a trial was taking place.

Two old men had come before the judge, and had accused a beautiful young woman named Susannah of a terrible crime. The judges, after listening to all that the old men had to say, condemned Susannah to death. The executioners were about to lead her away, when Daniel suddenly arose, and said that the old men were the real culprits and that they had tried to make Susannah do wrong; that, as she was a very good woman, she refused to do so, and the old men, in anger, had decided to punish her for not doing as they wished, by telling a lie to the judges.

When Daniel had spoken thus, the judges gazed upon the old men, whose guilty faces proved that he had told the truth. So the old men were condemned, and Susannah was allowed to go free. She was honored everywhere after this as a truly good woman.

Daniel's career after he had been saved from the lions' den seems to have been very prosperous. He spoke many prophecies, which are written down in the book bearing his name, and he foretold that at the end of seventy weeks the captive Jews would be allowed to go back to Jerusalem. He added that their hopes would finally be crowned by the coming of the long-promised Messiah, the Prince of Peace.

Daniel also had many visions, among which was one of four beasts. The first was like a lion with eagle's wings, the second like a bear, the third like a leopard, with four wings and four heads, and lastly came another beast, different from all the rest, and with ten horns on its head. This strange vision, like the statue which Nebuchadnezzar had seen, was interpreted as a sign of the kingdoms which would rule the land in turn; and it has been called a prophecy of coming political events.

Cyrus the Great, having finished all his conquests, now came back to rule in person over Babylon; and there he soon made a law which allowed the Jewish captives to go back to Jerusalem, and he also gave them permission to rebuild their famous temple.

A great-grandson of King Jehoiakim was chosen by Cyrus to lead the Jews home, and a long caravan was soon formed, numbering forty-two thousand three hundred and sixty men. Among these was Jeshua, the high priest, to whom were intrusted all the golden vessels carried away from Jerusalem so many years before, and plenty of money to build a new temple.

As soon as the Jews came to Jerusalem, they offered up sacrifices, and began rebuilding both the city and the temple. They were greatly hindered in this work, however, by the constant raids of their neighbors, whose proffered services had been refused because they were idolaters.

As one half of the Jews were obliged to be always under arms and on the watch to drive back these enemies, the work went on very slowly. Then, long before the temple was finished, Cyrus died, and when a new king came to the throne, he sent them strict orders to stop their labors.

Two of the Hebrew prophets finally obtained the repeal of this order, and, setting vigorously to work, the Jews finished their new temple five hundred and fifteen years before Christ.

CHAPTER LXVI

THE STORY OF ESTHER

THE next Persian king who claims our attention is Xerxes, who is called Ahasuerus in the Bible. This monarch had married a beautiful princess named Vashti. Proud of her beauty, he once bade her appear unveiled before his courtiers; but as such a thing seemed immodest to an Eastern woman, she refused to obey him.

The Persian king, whose orders had never before been disregarded, was so angry at Vashti for this refusal that he vowed he would never see her again. He soon regretted these rash words, for he loved her dearly; but as the words of a Persian king could never be taken back, he could not recall her.

His courtiers, seeing him sad and lonely, now suggested that the most beautiful maidens from all parts of his realm should be brought together, so that he might make choice of a new wife among them. The king was pleased by this suggestion; but as some time would be needed before it could be carried out, he spent the time of waiting by making his great expedition against Greece.[1]

On his return, the maidens were assembled, and he picked out from among them all a beautiful young Jewess named Esther, the niece of Mordecai, one of his government officers. Soon after the marriage had taken place, Mordecai made known to Esther a secret plot against the king's life, and thus helped him to seize and punish the men who would have liked to murder him.

The account of this service, and the name of the man who rendered it, were written down in the annals of the king's reign; for, like the other Persian monarchs, Ahasuerus kept a record of all that was done in his kingdom.

There was at the court, at this time, another foreigner, Haman the Amalekite, a cunning, cruel, and envious man. He hated all the Jews because they had been the enemies of his race, and he felt a special dislike for Mordecai, because this man had refused to show him the respect which he fancied was his due.

Haman, having reached the rank of prime minister and special adviser of the king, soon persuaded his master that the Jews in his kingdom were plotting a revolt. Thus he obtained from Ahasuerus a decree ordering a general massacre of all the Jews in his territory on a certain date.

In the time between the making and carrying out

[1]See Guerber's *Story of the Greeks.*

of this decree, the news came to the ears of Mordecai. He was in despair when he heard that he and all his unhappy race were doomed to die. In his grief, he tore his clothes and put ashes upon his head, which was the usual sign of mourning among the Jews at that time.

Then Mordecai went to sit at the palace gates, where some of the servants of Esther saw him. They went and told the queen that her uncle was out there, in deep grief. So Esther sent to ask what was the matter, and thus heard of the terrible decree which Haman had obtained from the king. She too was in despair, and when Mordecai said that she must go to her husband and plead for herself and for her people, she said that it was impossible.

It seems that no one in the whole Persian court was allowed to appear before the king without being called. If any one, even his wife, came into his presence unasked, the guards drew their swords and killed that person on the spot, unless the king stretched out his scepter to the visitor.

Urged by Mordecai, Esther finally said that she would risk her life to save her people, and, after spending some time in prayer, she dressed herself in her finest clothes, so that her beauty might help her to win the king's favor. Then she went into the king's room, but when she caught a glimpse of his stern face, she almost fainted with terror.

Ahasuerus now saw who it was that had dared to come into his presence without being asked. Touched by Esther's great beauty and entreating gestures, he not only forgave her for coming, but promised to grant any favor she might ask, even to the half of his kingdom.

Esther timidly said that if he would only honor her by coming to a feast in her rooms, to which Haman was also to be asked, she would tell him what wish had driven her into his presence at the risk of her life.

The king promised to come, and when Esther had gone, he called Haman and invited him to supper in his wife's name. Haman was delighted, for this was a very great honor; but as he left the palace he saw Mordecai, who again refused to bow down before him.

This second refusal made Haman so angry that he followed his wife's advice, and had a gallows built over seventy-five feet high. He meant to get the king's permission to hang Mordecai upon these gallows on the morrow, because he was too impatient for his revenge to wait until the day named for the killing of all the Jews.

CHAPTER LXVII

THE JEWS SAVED FROM DEATH

O N the night after Esther's visit, it happened that the king was very restless, and could not sleep. So he called one of his servants and bade him read aloud the annals of his reign. Ahasuerus listened, well pleased, until the man came to the part which told of the king's danger, and how he had been saved from death by Mordecai's warning.

The king, thus reminded of this great service, quickly asked what reward had been given to the man who had saved him. When the servant answered that nothing had been done for Mordecai, Ahasuerus was very indignant, and called for some one to advise him what reward would be best. The servant went in search of a courtier, and found Haman, who had come to the palace very early, so that he could get an order to hang Mordecai.

As soon as he was brought into the king's presence, Ahasuerus cried, "What shall be done unto the man whom the king delighteth to honor?"

Like the vain man that he was, Haman fancied that the reward could be intended only for himself; so he promptly answered that the man ought to be clad in royal robes, and set upon one of the king's own horses. Then some noble prince ought to lead the horse by the bridle through the principal streets of the city, calling aloud to all the people to bow down before the king's faithful servant.

Delighted with this answer, Ahasuerus told Haman to call Mordecai, and have him richly dressed, and mounted upon the best horse in the royal stables. The king added that Haman, as the greatest person at court, should lead the horse by the bridle and do all that he had said.

Haman's heart was full of rage when he heard this, and he hated Mordecai worse than ever. Still he did not dare to disobey, and had to do all as he had said. But as he bade the people bow down before Mordecai, he kept thinking that his turn would soon come; for the day named for the massacre of the Jews was near at hand.

When evening came, Haman went to the palace to attend the queen's feast, little thinking what awaited him there. The supper passed off well, and when it was nearly ended the king reminded Esther that she had not yet asked him the favor which he had promised to grant. Then Esther fell at the king's feet and told him that a traitor had plotted to bring about her death, and that of all her race. A few astonished questions on the king's part soon brought to light the whole story, and Ahasuerus, seeing Haman's baseness, condemned him to be hung on the gallows which had been built for Mordecai's execution.

As a royal decree could not be set aside in Persia, Ahasuerus now made another, warning all the Jews in his kingdom of their peril, and allowing them to defend themselves. The result of these two conflicting orders was a desperate armed struggle, in which seventy-five thousand Persians lost their lives. It was then that the Jews won the victory which they have celebrated ever since at a feast called Purim.

We know nothing further of the Jews, who were still in captivity, until Ezra got from another Persian monarch a permit to go to Jerusalem, with all the Jews who wished to accompany him thither. This new caravan reached the Holy City in safety, and Ezra is said to have made many reforms in the government of the people.

Some thirteen years later, when he was again in the city, Ezra was joined there by Nehemiah, another noted Jew, who, after visiting the place by night, decided to rebuild the old walls. Encouraged by his words and example, the Jews labored so hard that the work was soon done, in spite of the hindrances raised by their many enemies.

On another visit to Jerusalem, a few years later, Nehemiah purified the temple, made the people remember to keep the Sabbath holy, and began many other reforms. These are all written in the book bearing his name, which also contains many appeals to God to have mercy upon his Chosen People.

The last book in the Old Testament, and the last considered sacred by the Jews, is the book of the prophet

Malachi, "the voice of one crying in the wilderness." He preached repentance to the people, told them it was the only right way to get ready for the coming of the long-promised Messiah, and foretold the birth of John the Baptist, four hundred years before he came.

Although the Old Testament ends here and the New Testament begins more than four centuries later, we find in history a record of the principal events which happened to the Jews during those long years when first the Greeks and then the Romans became masters of the Old World.

CHAPTER LXVIII

ALEXANDER AND THE HIGH PRIEST

WHEN the Jews came back from captivity, they were under the rule of the high priest Jeshua, and although later on a Persian governor was sent to collect tribute, etc., the government was still a theocracy as of old. Shortly after Nehemiah's death, Judah, or Judea, was placed under the rule of a governor of Syria; but the Jews revolted before long, and then their land was again overrun by armies, and many of them were carried off into captivity.

It was during the time of the high priest Jaddua the Sixth, after the return from captivity under Cyrus the Great, that Alexander, King of Macedon, crossed over into Asia Minor. He defeated the Persians in the battles of Granicus and Issus, and conquered all Asia Minor, Syria, and Phœnicia. Then he marched into Judea, where he wanted to punish the people for supplying his enemies with food and refusing to help him.

Warned in a dream, Jaddua, instead of getting ready to fight, opened wide the city gates, and clothed all the people in white. Then heading a long procession of priests in full dress, he went forth to meet the coming host.

Jaddua met Alexander at the head of his army; and, to the surprise of all present, the proud young conqueror jumped down from his horse and paid respectful homage to the high priest. When asked why he had thus suddenly forgotten his anger against the Jews, Alexander said that before he had set out from home he had been favored by a vision, in which Jaddua had appeared to him, inviting him to cross over into Asia, and foretelling his victory over the Persians.

Hand in hand, Alexander and Jaddua now went up to the temple, where the young conqueror asked the high priest to offer a sacrifice in his name. Alexander examined the temple with wonder, and heard the priests read out of their sacred books. The one he liked best was that of Daniel, where the high priest showed him how his coming had been foretold in Nebuchadnezzar's vision of the statue.

When Alexander the Great died at Babylon, a few years later, the vast empire which he had conquered was divided between his generals. The first ruler of Palestine, however, did not long keep it; for Ptolemy, King of Egypt, another of Alexander's generals, soon took possession of it by force.

As the Jews refused to obey him, Ptolemy marched against them; and, by attacking them only on the Sabbath Day, when they were forbidden by law to fight, he soon became their master. To punish them, he carried off one hundred thousand Jews into Egypt, where they formed the bulk of the population in some of the recently founded cities, among which was Alexandria.

Six years later, another claimant wrested Judea away from Ptolemy, but the Egyptians soon recovered possession of it. When peace was restored, Ptolemy II. asked the high priest to send seventy learned men to Alexandria, to make a Greek translation of the books of the Old Testament. These men performed their task with the utmost care, and produced a beautiful translation. From the number of men who worked at it, this version of the Old Testament is known as the Septuagint.

The King of Syria and his successors kept up a long and bloody warfare with the Kings of Egypt, for the possession of Judea; and after many ups and downs Ptolemy IV. entered Jerusalem, and tried to force his way into the temple's inmost sanctuary. Simon, the high priest, courageously forbade this desecration, and thereby so angered Ptolemy that he treated the conquered Jews with the greatest cruelty.

A few years later, the King of Syria was master of the Jews, and had to raise some money; so he sent one of his officers, named Heliodorus, to strip the temple of its gold and silver.

The people were terrified by the danger which threatened them; for they knew that they were not strong enough to defend this treasure. They groaned and prayed aloud, and it is said that when Heliodorus entered the temple, he was met by an angel of the Lord, mounted upon a fiery steed. This rider trampled him under foot, while two other angels, armed with whips, chastised him severely.

Heliodorus did not dare to make any further attempt to take the treasure; but at last it fell into the hands of the enemy.

Some years later, another general also desecrated the temple, by driving a herd of swine into its sacred courts. This was "the abomination of desolation" which the faithful Jews could neither forgive nor forget, and they gladly rallied around a bold leader, Mattathias, determined to make a brave stand for their religion, which the enemy would fain have stamped out for good.

CHAPTER LXIX

THE BEGINNING OF THE END

MATTATHIAS had noticed that by strictly keeping the Sabbath, his people had often been defeated; so he now led them into battle even on the holy day, and won so many victories that the Jews soon began to gain hope once more. When his end was drawing near, this brave old man called his five sons to his bedside. He named Simon, the second and wisest, as ruler and adviser, while Judas Maccabæus, the third, was made general of the army.

The Maccabees, as these five brethren and their descendants are generally called, fought so bravely that they little by little defeated all the generals sent against them. They became masters of Jerusalem, repaired the temple, and after purifying it again began to worship God in it.

It was at this time that a small vial of holy oil miraculously supplied enough for all the temple lamps; and ever since then the faithful Jews have commemorated this miracle by the "Feast of Lights."

The Maccabees went on fighting against the Syrians with the utmost bravery. For instance, one of them once slipped under a fighting elephant which he fancied carried the Syrian king, and sacrificed his own life in hopes of killing the enemy of his people.

Judas Maccabæus struggled without a pause for ten years, fighting more battles than we can count, and with only a small force keeping the enemy at bay until the Jews had a chance to rise from the dust. At the end of this time he fell in battle; but when he died it was knowing that he had done his best, and had taught his followers how to fight and be strong.

The Jews were now guided in turn by the other Maccabees, and under one of them they entirely shook off the Syrian dominion, and entered into a league with the Romans. At this time the province of Samaria was laid waste, and a rival temple there was destroyed.

Aristobulus, one of the Maccabees, was the first who bore the royal title since the return from Babylon, but his reign was very short. The next king left two sons, who quarreled over the throne, and one of them asked for the help of the Romans.

Pompey, the great Roman general, came in answer to this appeal, and although he entered Judea as an umpire, he staid there as a master, and forced the Jews to pay tribute to Rome. In the course of this war, the temple hill was besieged and taken by storm. Pompey entered the temple, and in spite of all remonstrances he forced his way into the Holy of Holies, where none but the high priest was allowed to enter, and that only once a year.

Pompey also pulled down the walls of Jerusalem,

which had been rebuilt by Nehemiah, but he allowed the Jews to continue their worship as before. Ten years later, Crassus, another Roman, came to Syria. He was very greedy for gold, and he ordered that the temple should be robbed and all its treasures carried off.

When Julius Cæsar became master of Rome, he appointed a governor for Judea; but this ruler was soon succeeded by his son Herod the Great, who took the title of king. To make the Jews friendly to him this Herod married Mariamne, sister of the high priest, and the last member of the royal family; but he finally murdered her and her sons in a fit of jealousy.

About twenty years before our era, Herod, hoping to disarm the wrath of the Jews, who still hated him, began to rebuild the ruined temple, and the main part of this work was finished the very year that Christ was born.

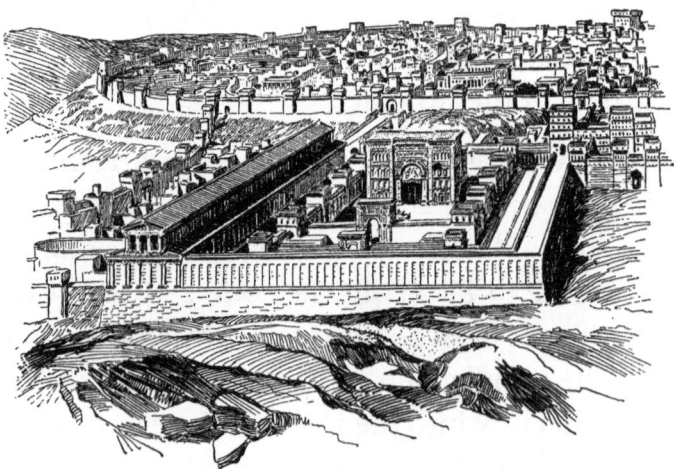

HEROD'S TEMPLE

CHAPTER LXX

THE DESTRUCTION OF JERUSALEM

YOU have seen, all through the course of this history, how anxiously the Chosen People had been watching and praying for the coming of the promised Messiah, the prince and deliverer. When you read and understand the prophecies where his coming is foretold, you will perhaps see why the Jews and Christians have different opinions on this subject.

The Jews were and are a proud and shrewd people, and it was very galling to them to be under the rule of foreigners. As the prophecies had told of a coming prince, and had described his power and glory, the Jews expected—and still expect—a mighty earthly king.

The Christians, in reading the same prophecies, see that the long-promised Messiah was indeed a king, but one whose kingdom was not of the earth, and short-lived, but of heaven, and eternal. These two very different explanations of the sayings of the prophets have been the cause of many disputes.

In the days of Herod, the faithful Jews were very

much excited; because, as far as they could make out, it was now about time for the promised Messiah to appear. Now, all of you who have Christian parents are familiar with the story of Jesus Christ,—the Messiah, according to the Christians. You know that his coming had been foretold to his mother, Mary, by an angel, that he was born in Bethlehem, in a manger, and that an angel announced his birth to some poor shepherds, who were the first to worship him.

You have also heard how three wise men came from the East to Jerusalem, following a star, and asking: "Where is he that is born King of the Jews?" This question came to the ears of Herod; and as he was afraid that the prophecies might be true, he ordered the massacre of all the innocent little children in Bethlehem.

The infant Jesus, as you know, was not killed with the rest, because Joseph, warned by an angel, had gone with him and his mother to Egypt. The story of the life of Jesus, which you will find in the New Testament, tells how he came back to Palestine when Herod died, how he grew up at Nazareth, and how he visited the temple at Jerusalem when he was only twelve years old.

Next we find there an account of the teaching and preaching of Christ, whom Christians consider the son of God, while Mussulmans think he was a prophet, and the Jews call him an impostor. The Jews were very angry that a poor man should be called the Messiah, and this is the reason why they accused Christ of blasphemy, and, with the help of the Romans, crucified him.

In the course of his teaching and preaching, Christ

had foretold—as had many of the prophets before him—that Jerusalem would be destroyed before very long. These words had only served to make the Jews angrier still, because they loved their city, and could not bear to think that any harm would happen to it.

After Christ's death, resurrection, and ascension, which are also related in the New Testament, many people believed that he was the promised Messiah, the son of God, and began to worship him. Because they did so, they were persecuted by the Jews and by the Romans; and they were finally driven out of Jerusalem, and went to live elsewhere.

The historians of this time tell us that the Jews were quarreling among themselves, that every man's hand was against his brother, and that strange signs and prodigies showed that the end was very near. A comet hung over the city, chariots and armies were seen in the sky, and all hearts were filled with a nameless fear.

The Jews, in terror, now suddenly revolted against the Romans. The latter sent large armies to Palestine, under their generals Titus and Vespasian, and captured town after town. Finally Titus came and laid siege to Jerusalem, which was in the hands of several different political parties, and surrounded by three great walls.

So many people had taken refuge in the city that there was soon a most horrible famine. Then, too, the Roman engines threw showers of stones, arrows, and burning pitch into the city. After a most heroic resistance, Jerusalem was taken, inch by inch; and, as the people fought to the very end, and would not surrender, they were nearly all killed.

The temple was taken last, and having been accidentally set on fire, this magnificent building was entirely burned. Titus only managed to save the golden vessels and candlestick, which were carried by his soldiers in his triumph on his return to Rome.

The walls of Jerusalem were razed, a Roman garrison was placed there, and all the Jews that were left were sent away, and were told that they would be put to death if they ever came back.

Thus driven out of their native country, for many years the Jews scattered all over the world; but wherever they went they carried with them the story of their race, which has been briefly told you in this little volume.

www.ingramcontent.com/pod-product-compliance
Lightning Source LLC
Chambersburg PA
CBHW021046090426
42738CB00006B/202